Jewish Life in Canada

Jewish Life in Canada

Paintings & Commentaries by William Kurelek
A Historical Essay by Abraham Arnold

Hurtig Publishers/Edmonton/1976

Hurtig Publishers
10560 105 Street
Edmonton, Alberta

ISBN 0-88830-107-3

All the paintings in this book are in the collection
of Mr. and Mrs. Jules Loeb.

Printed and bound in Canada

Contents

For Vanessa and Manya

Introduction

I first got the idea for this series in 1973. It was meant to express my thanks to the Jewish community for their important part in my success as an artist. It was Avrom Isaacs, a Jew, who first discovered me and took the risk of exhibiting my work. After ten years of my trying in vain on my own for recognition he gave me that necessary break. In fact, he gave me two opening nights. The first was sponsored by a Jewish women's organization. They bought a few of my pictures too. Jewish art collectors were my first patrons, followed hard by those of British origin; and Av Isaacs has been actively promoting my work ever since.

However, to my surprise, when I began making this project about them known to the Jewish community there was no immediate interest. In fact, I seemed to sense embarrassment and hesitation. Also surprising to me was the fact that though the Jewish community is noted for being relatively well-to-do, their museums here in Canada were just struggling into existence.

The two best helpers and morale supporters in this project turned out to be the two Abes of Winnipeg — Abe Schwartz, an engineer working for TransCanada Pipelines, and Abe Arnold, a Canadian Jewish historian. These two gave unstintingly in time and effort. I spent an intensive two days of research and briefing with them — and this in the face of a fierce Manitoba blizzard that hit Winnipeg just then.

The actual execution of the paintings took place during my most recent pilgrimage to Lourdes. The location may seem rather odd to my Jewish friends, but to me it seems quite appropriate since that is where hundreds of miraculous cures attributed to the intercession of Mary, a Jewish maiden, have taken place. It ties in, too, with another reason I had for doing the series. I wanted to do my bit in undoing some of the injustices Jews have suffered at the hands of Christians. That takes a little courage, I found, since there is still anti-Semitism around, sometimes just below the surface. It is easy to condemn the Spanish Inquisition (which persecuted Jews as well as Protestants) as evil or misguided. Such Christianity is a hideous mockery of the Founder's aims. As a believing Christian I am convinced Christ was the Messiah that the Jews, who were God's chosen people, were expecting but, nevertheless, it still doesn't make sense to me that the descendants of the Jews of Christ's time should be persecuted. It is one thing to disagree with someone; it is quite another to force him to accept your beliefs.

Modern anti-Semitism is more difficult to understand. There's the kind I've experienced among my own people for example. I've been hearing conflicting versions of the old-country Jew and gentile situation all my life and stories of injustices on both sides.

But then there is Nazi anti-Semitism. At an ecumenical prayer meeting I recently attended it was pointed out by one of the leaders that it had been a supposedly Christian country, Germany, that systematically murdered six million Jews. The shame of that crime is shared in some part by Christians throughout the world. As a Christian I hope through my art to help in paying the debt we are in as a result of that enormous crime.

I certainly don't agree with perpetuating feuds and racial hostilities anywhere, especially so in Canada. Here we can at least show respect for and interest in another people's traditions. It's to that end that I included half a dozen cultural heritage subjects in this series.

William Kurelek

Jewish Immigrants Arriving on the Prairies

Jewish farm settlement in the West predates all other farm groups except the British, French, Icelandic and Mennonite settlements. Canadian immigration policy gave British and North Europeans prime preference and gave central and eastern Europeans, which included most Jews, second class preference. Often Jews didn't even get secondary treatment.

When the Jews immigrated as farmers they gave farming a try; if it didn't work they were prepared to do something else — peddling, tailoring or various other trades and crafts. Jews usually came with a more varied occupational and cultural background than immigrants from other ethnic groups that were mostly of peasant stock. Jews were, by tradition, more mobile and occupationally more versatile. These qualities were not considered desirable by Canadian immigration authorities in the days of the opening of the West; when Jews arrived in the West in 1882 they found a confused immigration policy working against them and no land allotted for them.

In this painting the group on the station platform are heading for the established Jewish farm colony at Sonnenfeld, Saskatchewan (c. 1920). They are somewhat dazed by the emptiness of the new land as they wait for a colony family to come and fetch them by horse wagon. I have put the lady in front by herself not because she is anti-social, but to bring her closer to gallery visitors who would then see the shifskart ("ship ticket") she is clinging to. This was like a passport to freedom and economic opportunity for each new Jewish immigrant to Canada, after the persecution and feeling of being unwanted in Europe.

I have talked with former Jewish farming people in Winnipeg and with Larry Zolf in Toronto about these farm colonists. Larry maintains that the colonies were nationalistically inspired efforts to prove that Jews could farm. Pioneer descendants of the Edenbridge settlers denied this, however. I don't know which view is correct. I do know I need no proof of Jewish ability to make a living off the land, for I have personally seen the amazing progress the Israelis are making on the kibbutzim and in other projects greening the deserts in Israel.

Pioneering at Edenbridge, Saskatchewan

Edenbridge, founded in 1906, was one of several successful Jewish farm colonies in Canada. A group of about twenty Jewish immigrants who had left their homes in Lithuania at the turn of the century and emigrated to South Africa, were inspired to make a second migration, this time to the new province of Saskatchewan in western Canada, when they read a 1905 pamphlet issued by the Department of Immigration offering each settler 160 acres of virgin land for ten dollars. They rejected the idea of settling on lands near the established Jewish farm colonies at Hirsch and Lipton because these areas had very few trees. Instead they picked a densely wooded district along the Carrot River north of Star City. It took much imagination to see this as a panorama of cultivated fields and flourishing crops; it took years of back-breaking toil and seemingly endless troubles to turn the vision into a reality.

When the settlement was granted a post office the farmers discussed a possible name for it. Sam Vickar, one of the most socially active settlers, records the meeting in his diary. "We all wanted to call it 'Jewish Bridge' after the bridge that spanned the Carrot River here, but we thought perhaps the postmaster general might not agree. We read through the list of post office names in the Canadian postal guide and found many names beginning with Eden. So we made a quick and unanimous decision that the name of the new post office should be Edenbridge." A quick decision was made possible because *Yidden* in the Yiddish language means Jews.

The Edenbridge synagogue was built in 1908 and served as a house of worship until 1964. Edenbridge also had a community hall and two public schools, as well as Hebrew, Yiddish and religious classes, a dramatic society and a Jewish newspaper published at irregular intervals.

I have tried to incorporate twenty-five years of development into this one picture. For example, a farmer is plowing with oxen in the field, but by the house a family is cutting firewood with a saw powered by a steam engine. We also see efforts to "thicken the pot" within the limits of dietary laws by fishing in the Carrot River, trapping animals and birds and picking mushrooms. Also shown are efforts to improve and extend the crop-bearing fields by picking stones, clearing timber and burning underbrush. Near the farm house are two small buildings which we wouldn't find at a gentile neighbours' farm, the Mikvah, a ritual bathhouse used by Orthodox Jewish women to purify themselves after their menstrual periods, and the sukkah, a temporary building used during the Sukkot thanksgiving festival in the fall of the year as a reminder of the temporary dwellings used by the ancient Israelites during their forty years of wandering in the Sinai wilderness.

Bender Hamlet, the Farming Colony that Failed

Edenbridge, Saskatchewan, was one of a half dozen Jewish farm colonies, started on the prairies around 1900 that flourished for fifty years or longer. The others were at Hirsch, Sonnenfeld, Wapella and Lipton in Saskatchewan and at Rumsey and Trochu in Alberta. Some Jews tried farming at Montefiore in Alberta and Camper, Pine Ridge and Bender Hamlet in Manitoba, for ten, fifteen or even twenty years but then they gave up and drifted into Winnipeg and other cities.

Bender Hamlet, the first Jewish farm colony in Manitoba, was started in 1903 in the Interlake district seventy miles northeast of Winnipeg. The settlers soon found that much of the land was stony and short of water. Drinking water had to be hauled by oxcart from a common well. Those who stuck it out longest left the area with many memories, both happy and sad ones.

It is these memories that I have fitted into the panel of the frame as black pen and ink drawings. My Winnipeg friend, Abe Schwartz, sent me his great-aunt's diary describing her adventures farming in North Dakota. I snipped the pages into convenient pieces and incorporated them into the frame as well. I want to convey the idea that these memories are like voices in the wind as it sighs through the thistles of the overgrown fields and through the chinks of abandoned buildings.

As a matter of special interest I should point out that the joyful hunting and shooting related by Abe Schwartz's great-aunt would have been frowned on by, say, a Jewish colonist at Wapella, Saskatchewan. There they stuck to the more Orthodox dietary laws that forbade eating unkosher meat. They had to trap their animals live first and so could not obtain their meat in such an easy manner as described by Abe's great-aunt.

Jewish Scrap Collector Questioned by a Toronto Policeman

This picture of an old Toronto street and a Jewish peddler wagon is a composite from memories gathered during my one year of art school in Toronto back in 1949-50, and from three scenes from Jewish archives photos. One of these photographs is of a scrap metal collector in Moose Jaw, Saskatchewan; one is of a Jewish street peddler with a pushcart; the third photograph is one of a rag-and-bones man being questioned by a policeman. The last two photographs date to about 1910 in Toronto.

To a struggling Jewish immigrant it appeared a step up the economic ladder to have accumulated enough money to purchase a horse and cart for peddling or collecting and selling scrap. Many such new entrepreneurs spoke broken English and were regarded with suspicion by the community — I've even heard cases of mothers who used to frighten children into obedience by threatening to give them away to the scrap man. These men used to come out to our farm in Manitoba to buy cowhides and rabbit skins to sell in Winnipeg. In this picture perhaps he is being questioned about possession of a peddler's licence.

14

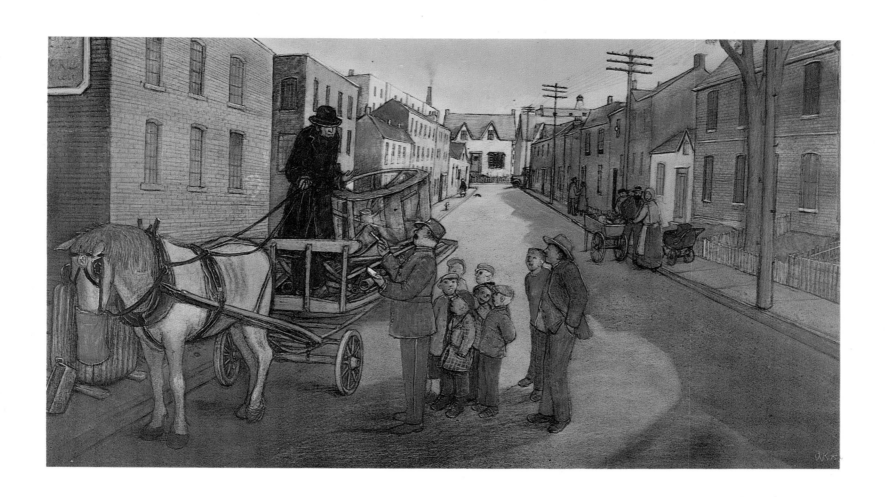

General Store in Vancouver Before World War One

Just as the Chinese in Canada were often thought of as laundry men and restaurateurs the Jews have usually been regarded as traders. Fredelle Bruser Maynard has written a most revealing book about her storekeeper father's life on the Canadian prairies in *Raisins and Almonds*. Actually he didn't live up to the stereotype public concept of the prosperous, sharp dealing Jewish business man; he went from failure to failure. Today there are few small Jewish stores left if for no other reason than that they, like other small entrepreneurs, have been forced out of business by big chain stores and supermarkets. *Raisins and Almonds* describes that with sympathy and insight.

Many Jews pioneered in the commercial development of the West. In towns and villages throughout the prairies the first store was often opened by a Jewish merchant. It was invariably a general store and became an important community institution in the decades when communication was still fairly primitive. Many general store operators came to play a role in the community sometimes more important than their function as merchants. The Jewish general store proprietor could usually speak several languages of the old country. He therefore served his customers not only with needed merchandise, but as a translator in dealing with the government, as a postmaster, and generally as a centre for the exchange of community news and information.

Jewish Dairy Farm Outside Winnipeg

In the Stonewall district north of Winnipeg there is a marginal,
partly boggy, farming area more suited to dairying than to grain
farming. People from all nationalities settled in it — my father
was one — and at least a dozen of the dairymen there were Jews.
Two that we knew were Goodman Glow and Farmer Steele.
(Mr. Steele's daughter, Mira, married Sidney Spivak, the former
leader of the Conservative opposition in the Manitoba legislature.) Homely details in this painting, such as the puppies
wrestling in the grass, the swallows winging their gyroscopic
way about the barn door, and the cat and kittens waiting for
their saucer of milk are drawn from my own memories. My little
daughter Cathy, who is one of my art critics and an aspiring
veterinarian, says the kittens are really mice because of the shape
of their ears.

Jews in the Clothing Business in Winnipeg

Many of the Jews settling in Winnipeg's north end were from Poland, Russia and the Ukraine where, partly as a result of czarist laws that forbade them to own land, they often went into trades and became tailors, blacksmiths, merchants and tavern keepers. When Jewish tailors left eastern Europe to settle here it was quite natural for them to move to the booming garment centers of Montreal, Toronto and Winnipeg where they worked in, or sometimes were founders of, both manufacturing and retail garment businesses. It might have been a one man tailor shop, or a father-son partnership, or a somewhat larger business, as in this picture. Often a small outfit, following the lead of supply and demand, might develop into what is called a "sweat shop" garment factory such as one seen through the window in this painting.

When Jewish settlers arrived in the West during the 1880s and early 1900s, they were unaware that powerful eastern interests were trying to preserve the West as a consumer area for goods manufactured in the East, and many went into some kind of manufacturing. When the Hirsch colony was founded, a discussion started as to what those settlers would do all winter.

There is a proposal recorded in the files of the Baron de Hirsch Institute in Montreal that each homestead family be equipped with a sewing machine to produce its own clothing during the winter months. According to this plan it would be necessary to erect in the colony "a building large enough to cut the goods, give them out to be made, receive them back, showroom and shipping room . . . ." As far as is known the Hirsch factory was never started. However, other Jews who settled in Winnipeg did start a textile and clothing industry for western Canada. Thus the Jews played an important role in changing the character of the West from a preserve for eastern interests into an area that began to develop its own secondary industry.

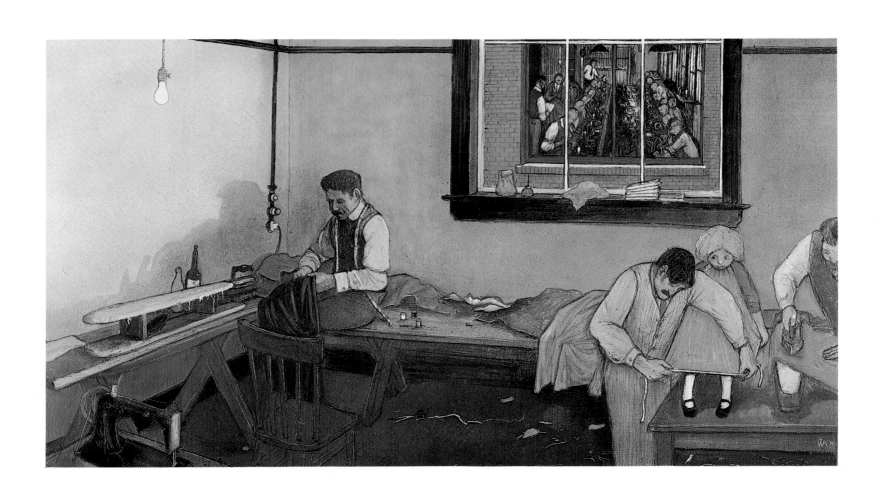

Baker's Family Celebrating the Sabbath in Edmonton

I once worked in Edmonton as a construction worker where I put
in sidewalk curbs, so I got acquainted with such western back
lanes as the one seen in the light of the setting sun through the
window in this painting. A Jewish Sabbath day begins at sundown just as it is recorded in Genesis. Father is away at the
pre-Sabbath synagogue service, but mother has to have the
meal ready because, belonging as she does to the Orthodox
synagogue, she cannot work on the Sabbath. She lights the
ceremonial candles as the children watch her and recites the
words: "Blessed art Thou O Lord, our God, King of the universe,
who hast sanctified us through Thy commandments and commanded us to kindle the Sabbath lights."

Since the father is a baker, the ceremonial bread (challah)
will be the best. On the table and the sideboard, which holds the
extras, are seen the main dishes: gefilte fish, which are cold fish
patties with sliced carrots, served with grated horseradish and
beets as Ukranians make them; chicken soup; boiled chicken;
sea shell noodles with buckwheat kashe; knishes, which are like
Ukranian perogy, stuffed with potato; and red wine. No milk or
butter is allowed. For dessert there could be honey cake or kugel,
which is a noodle cake. Poorer families would not have all this
variety. But rich or poor the father in an Orthodox family is
regarded as king; only after he has sat at the head of the table,
blessed his family and table by saying, "May the Lord bless you
and keep you on this Sabbath day," can the meal begin.

Jewish Doctor's Family Celebrating Passover in Halifax

I visualized this Seder celebrated in Halifax to indicate how widespread Jewish settlement is across the country and how often Jews are found in important professions like medicine, education, law and government. I have shown a more Orthodox family than average so that I could incorporate a greater number of interesting customs. One, for example, is illustrated by the small boy searching in between the cushions on which his father is reclining for half a matzah which the doctor has pretended to hide from him. When the boy finds this special matzah (afikomon), in this search game, he will hide it and later redeem it for a gift. Traditionally the Passover meal cannot be completed without the afikomon. Any of the children may take part in this game.

Some heads of the house dress totally in white but here I have painted only a white prayer shawl draped around the doctor's collar. It is the tradition to invite relatives and friends so that the Seder becomes a large family gathering. At the centre of the table is the Seder plate holding three cakes of matzah, surrounded by ceremonial dishes: a roasted egg, a shank bone bitter herbs (horseradish), charoses (symbolizing the mortar for the bricks made by the Israelite slaves in ancient Egypt), and parsley or other greens.

The youngest child asks the father the four traditional questions from the Haggadah, of which each member has a copy beside his plate. These questions pretty well sum up the meaning and mood of the Passover Seder.

Why is tonight different from all other nights of the year —

in regard to the eating of unleavened bread?
in the use of bitter herbs?
in the ritual of dipping food in saltwater?
in the custom of reclining at the Seder table?

The story the father unfolds, read from the Haggadah, is the familiar tale of Egyptian slavery, Pharaoh's obstinate refusal to let the Israelites go, Moses' courageous leadership and the Miracle of Redemption. It is a happy occasion!

Jewish Home Life in Montreal

This picture depicts a scene from the early twenties. In the foreground the housewife is busy in the part of the house then regarded as her preserve in Orthodox homes, the kitchen and nursery. She is preparing blintzes, a pancake rolled with cheese or blueberry stuffing; or she may be making knishes, stuffed with meat or potato; or strudel, a delicious pastry. One of her daughters helps to stir the pot, but it must be the right pot depending on whether a meat or dairy dish is being prepared. (One set of pots and dishes is used for meat foods and a separate set for dairy meals. When a strictly Orthodox family eats meat there must be an interval of at least six hours before dairy foods may be eaten.)

Past this scene one can see children at various studies. Jews have always been aware of the power of education and encourage their children to shine. They encourage development in the arts, too, as can be seen by the young lad struggling to master the violin. On the dresser cupboard there are ceremonial religious objects, a tree of life, a nine-branch Chanukah candelabra and a Havdalah spice box used in the Sabbath-ending ceremony. On the doorjamb, to the right of the entrance from the kitchen, is fixed a mezuzah, a small case containing an inscription from Deuteronomy 6:4-9 and 11:13-21 and beginning, "Hear, O Israel: The Lord our God is one Lord."

In the study, beyond the children at work, a Torah study group in prayer shawls pores over a sacred text. Only men take part in such study groups which may be held in a home or in the synagogue.

Teperman's Wrecking Firm in Toronto

Jewish people are found in all kinds of businesses and professions; I could have chosen to illustrate any one out of the wide variety of these, but I settled for this particular business because I hoped thereby to show how Jews prospered in their newly adopted country.

Often small beginnings led quite naturally to larger enterprises. The scrap man we saw in illustration 11 may have been astute enough to go into the wrecking business himself. Not only would he pick up more scrap from the wreckage of a building, often he would not have to pay for it. In fact, he'd be paid to do the wrecking! At first he'd have only a few men to help, but as he tackled the wrecking of ever bigger buildings he would acquire more men, bigger machines and bigger acreage for his scrap yards. I once visited the Teperman yards in north Toronto when I needed a few pieces of used plywood. It was enormous. Another Jewish wrecking business I know of is Greenspoon Bros., the next largest in Toronto.

Morosnick's Market, Dufferin Street, Winnipeg

Many Jews had a tendency, probably picked up from their European backgrounds, of either originating or involving themselves energetically in indoor-outdoor market areas in big cities. Kensington Market in Toronto is a good example; at one time it was even called Jewish Market. Now Jews have migrated north to the Bathurst and Lawrence areas and their places have been filled by Portuguese, Hungarian and Chinese shopkeepers.

I've already painted Kensington Market; so for a change, here I've painted the old Winnipeg Dufferin Street market, where in the twenties Jewish vegetable peddlers did a lot of trading. However, I've included three stock Jewish market characters from photos of Toronto markets at the turn of the century: a shochet ("ritual slaughterer"), the one in a white apron carrying out a bunch of chickens; the necktie pedlar and the bakery delivery man.

These markets used to fascinate me and still do, and Jewish customs and traditions in them add to the flavour. For example, one could see live chickens in the window of a kosher butcher shop, or, in Montreal, a bagel factory in operation. In these markets one would often see the Chasidic Jew, who looked like a direct transfer from nineteenth century Poland with his long beard and black hat and sideburn locks.

Yom Kippur

For the sin which we have committed against Thee
under stress or through choice;

For the sin which we have committed against Thee
in stubbornness or in error;

For the sin which we have committed against Thee
in the evil meditations of the heart;

For the sin which we have committed against Thee
by word of mouth;

For the sin which we have committed against Thee
by abuse of power;

For the sin which we have committed against Thee
by exploiting and dealing treacherously with our neighbour;

For all these sins, O God of forgiveness, bear with us,
pardon us, forgive us!

This is the prayer which runs through the entire service on Yom Kippur, the Day of Atonement, which is the holiest day of Judaism. It is the last of the Ten Days of Penitence which begin with Rosh Hashanah. Yom Kippur is marked by twenty-four hours of prayer and fasting. White, symbol of purity, is the dominant colour of this solemn day. The altar cloths and Torah covers in the synagogue, maroon on the Sabbaths and blue on the festivals, are changed to white. The Kol Nidre chant, led by the cantor, is the prelude to the Day of Atonement and is recited just before the sun sets. It is a prayer for absolution, asking God for release from vows undertaken but not fulfilled. These vows refer only to man's promises to God — not to his fellow man. All the prayers of Yom Kippur cannot absolve a man from sins against his neighbour, only a forgiving neighbour can do so.

Rosh Hashanah is Hebrew for New Year. It marks one of the most sacred holy days in the Jewish faith and ushers in the Ten Days of Penitence when mankind passes in judgment before the heavenly throne. It is the period when Jews sit in judgment over themselves, comparing their personal conduct during the past year with the hopes and resolutions they had cherished. The most important symbol of the Rosh Hashanah and Yom Kippur observances is the shofar, or ram's horn, which is sounded during worship on the New Year and each of the Ten Days of Penitence. In the Rosh Hashanah services, the shofar is the call to worship. It calls upon the faithful to repent for their misdeeds of the past year.

Depending on how Orthodox or Reform a Jew is he will act out his remorse more or less emotionally. Though I've never seen this rite, I gather that, at the sounding of the shofar, each man does his own thing as far as expressing remorse. This ritual was, until very recently, practiced by Roman Catholics, when they would ceremoniously beat their breasts at the confiteor.

The synagogue interior used for this painting is the Kiever Synagogue in downtown Toronto. I also used a photograph of a painting given to me by the Jewish archives. In the one Sabbath service I attended I noticed Jews are more relaxed than Christians in their house of worship, sometimes walking around or turning to talk to their neighbours as the mood strikes them.

A Zionist Society in Montreal Honouring its University Grads

Jews have always been keen on higher learning and either push
or encourage their children to go as far as possible. Fredelle
Maynard describes this motivation well in *Raisins and Almonds*.
I have witnessed it myself, in high school and university in
Winnipeg and in Israel when I visited a professor at
the University of Jerusalem and his family.

To plan this painting I called on my recollection of a Ukranian community celebration in Montreal to honour the
community's high school graduates. I also used a photograph
of Jewish scholars that belonged to a Zionist fraternity on a
Montreal campus as they posed in their graduation gowns.

The Zionist movement, I gather, is both a religious and a political movement. The political efforts which led to the creation
of the new Jewish state began about eighty years ago. Since the
middle of the nineteenth century, Jews of eastern Europe living
under the rigours of czarist tyranny saw in Palestine the only
answer to their age-old problem of homelessness, but at first,
western European Jews had little sympathy for the idea.
However, when they discovered that emancipation had not
rooted out the evil of anti-Semitism, many became disillusioned
and gathered around a young Viennese journalist, Doctor
Theodor Herzel, who is considered the father of Zionism.
The official Zionist movement was formally organized in 1897.
Although its followers were united in general purpose, they
differed in their specific interests. Some felt that Palestine was a
refuge for the oppressed; others hoped that it would bring about
a rebirth of Jewish culture and the Hebrew language. Religious
Jews believed that in a homeland of their own they could adhere
to the rituals of their faith more fully; still others saw in Zionism a
safeguard against assimilation.

Jewish Separate School in Winnipeg

This painting is based on a photograph taken in 1922 of the Talmud Torah School in Winnipeg and on my experience of our one-room schoolhouse in Manitoba. Now that my own children attend a Catholic separate school, I believe I have more insight into the separate character of such Jewish schools.

The main characteristics are that religion is taught as a serious subject, and that the whole philosophy or outlook on the secular subjects is God-centred. There are, however, reasons for not classing Jewish private day schools as parochial. They are not attached to parishes or synagogues. They are financed largely by tuition fees and private contributions. Many of the teachers are secular. Half a day is devoted to standard public school subjects; the remainder of the curriculum is given over to religious and Jewish history studies. There is division among Jews on the subject of separate schools; the vast majority attend public schools.

Besides the philosophical difference between a Jewish and a gentile school, there are a few obvious external differences. For example, in most Jewish schools, the teacher, if a man, and each boy wear a skull cap (yarmulkah), the traditional male head-covering. There are Jewish charts and mottos on the walls and Hebrew script is in evidence. In some schools boys and girls are seated in separate rows.

Jewish Wedding in Calgary

The building in the background is the old downtown synagogue. It no longer exists, having been demolished in an urban renewal program. The photograph from which I painted caught my eye because in the background skyline one sees the famed Husky Tower; a revealing juxtaposition of the old and the new. I used artist's licence in painting green grass around the synagogue. Wherever and whenever possible a Jewish wedding was preferably performed outdoors so that the only thing between the wedding couple and the open sky would be the canopy called the chuppah.

Some of the customs honoured at a Jewish wedding are tied in with religion; some are cultural accretions. For example, I almost had the couple in this painting jumping over a loaf of bread, but Stephen Speisman stopped me by pointing out that it was a Romanian custom only. So I settled for the more universal Jewish ritual of breaking glass, a symbolic reminder of the destruction of the Temple by the Romans in 70 A.D. (Many wedding parties take this in a lighter vein for it has the psychological advantage of providing joyful relief to the seriousness of the ceremony.)

Other traditional symbols and rites are the sipping of a cup of wine at the ceremony's beginning and end; the unadorned wedding band; and the religious marriage document called the ketubah. The canopy stands for the privacy newlyweds are entitled to and also adds a touch of royalty, for the couple are regarded as king and queen on that day.

Judaism insists that marriage is not just a private matter, but an occurrence with which the entire community has a concern. In old European Jewish communities, for example, every wedding was more than a family affair. If a bride was too poor to afford a trousseau, a collection was made on the eve of the Sabbath and the girl was outfitted. No wedding invitations were sent out because the entire community considered it a religious obligation to attend to bless the couple and to comment on the radiant beauty of the bride.

Jewish Life in Canada

Introduction

The ancestors of Canada's Jews lived in Europe for more than two thousand years where they developed a new language and built religious and educational centres. Wherever they lived, in Spain, France and England, in Holland and the German states, and later in Poland and Russia, the Jews put down roots and made a valuable contribution to commerce, to science and to freedom of thought, when granted the opportunity. Jewish people served faithfully any ruler or government that maintained a policy of tolerance towards them.

Almost inevitably, however, acceptance turned to repression, persecution and expulsion, and this repetitive pattern led to the image of the "wandering Jew." Jewish experience, often uniquely painful, always reflected the ebb and flow of European history.

Jews began to move from west to east when the Crusaders, en route to the Holy Land, attacked them as infidels and killed many of them. Ghetto segregation began in the sixteenth century, and repeated expulsions from western and central European countries spurred the movement eastward.

By the seventeenth century a few Jews began to find their way to the New World. The first Jews in North America were twenty-three refugees who arrived in 1654 from a South American Dutch colony which had been conquered by the Portuguese. In Canada the earliest Jewish settlers arrived about 1760, after the British conquest of Montreal in the Seven Year War.

In Europe by the eighteenth century more than two million Jews were living in Poland and other countries. Here they experienced a cultural renaissance which found its stronghold in the shtetl, the small-town home of many Jews. In the shtetl, Yiddish was mame-loshen, the folk tongue, a primary creation of the European experience. Hebrew was loshen kodesh, the sacred tongue of scholarship and prayer in the Beth Hamidrosh, the synagogue and house of study. In the market place on weekdays Jews bargained with their peasant neighbours in Polish or Ukrainian. Shtetl Jews were tailors, bakers and shoemakers, locksmiths, blacksmiths and bricklayers, carpenters and watchmakers. They were innkeepers, peddlers and dairymen, as well as scholars and rabbis. Some Jews even became farmers or managers of land estates, although they had been largely barred from the land since feudal times.

Nowhere, however, were the Jews immune from persecution. Following a different religion and speaking a language of their own, they were always separated from the people among whom they lived and thus became a convenient target of attack whenever there was need for a scapegoat. Special difficulties arose in the second half of the eighteenth century when Poland was partitioned and most of the Jews came under the rule of the Russian czar. Even before the partition most Polish Jews had been living in poverty. In 1791 a czarist decree restricted the Jews to the Pale of Settlement, a territorial ghetto. This marked the beginning of new hardships. Jews could not live in large cities without special permission. They were virtually barred from attendance at the gimnazium ("high school") or university, and young Jewish boys were conscripted into the Russian army for twenty-five years. By the 1860s legal and economic restrictions were followed by physical attacks, pogroms, and this began to stimulate a new movement of Jews to the West.

A.J. Arnold

Jewish Immigration

On Saturday evening, 13 May 1882, the officers of the Anglo-Jewish Association, Montreal Branch, met with representatives of the Ladies Hebrew Benevolent Society and the Young Men's Hebrew Benevolent Society to plan for the "hourly expected arrival" of 260 Russian Jewish refugees. They formed a joint committee and called a community conference for the next day, when the Jewish Emigration Aid Society was established. The new society immediately launched a fund-raising campaign and rented three warehouses for temporary shelter.

The Montreal Jewish community, which then numbered a little more than eight hundred, had been active in assisting immigrants since the early 1860s through the Young Men's Hebrew Benevolent Society. In Toronto the Jewish community, which then counted about five hundred, had become involved in immigrant aid in the mid-1870s when the Toronto Hebrew Benevolent Society was established.

After the assassination of Czar Alexander II of Russia in 1881, pogroms against the Jews followed in many cities, and an exodus began which led to the largest Jewish immigration wave to North America. Thus, for the first time, there was very substantial Jewish immigration into Canada.

Some forty years earlier, when there were already 15,000 Jews living throughout North America, there were only 154 Jews in Canada. This difference may be traced to the fact that the American colonies became a relatively open haven for Jews and other dissenters by the mid-seventeenth century, about one hundred years before Canada's doors were opened following the British conquest. In fact when Canada was part of New France, Jews and all non-Catholics were explicitly barred from settlement by a ruling introduced by Cardinal Richelieu in 1627. It was just twenty-seven years later, in 1654, that the first Jews settled at New Amsterdam, which later became New York.

From the latter date there were three periods of Jewish immigration to North America. First there was the Spanish period which lasted until 1725; then the German-Polish period, from 1725 to 1880; and finally the Russian-Polish period, from 1880 into the twentieth century.

In the first immigration period none of the Jews established themselves in Canada. An apt analogy may be drawn by imagining oneself on an ocean shore watching the tide roll in. Each wave travels a little higher up the shore and at the highest point a bit of driftwood may be deposited, but the next wave washes it out to sea again. That is what happened to the rare Jew who tried to reach Canada during the French regime.

There is, for example, the well-known story of the girl, Esther Brandeau, who arrived in Quebec in September 1738, on the ship *Saint Michel*. She was disguised as a boy and used the name Jacques la Fargue. After her true identity was discovered she resisted all efforts to be converted to Catholicism and was shipped back to France.

In the second immigration period the inshore tide is stronger. Continuing our analogy, the waves flow in further and deposit some twigs and a few logs that finally get left behind. That is how the first 154 Jews remained in Canada between 1760 and 1841. After that the tide becomes stronger yet, but the number of Jews reaching Canada still represents merely the furthest reach of each wave. By 1851 there were some 450 Jews living in Canada, compared to 50,000 in the U.S., and by 1881 there were approximately 2500 Jews in Canada, compared to 230,000 in the U.S.

During the third immigration period, the same quantitative relationship between Jewish immigration to the United States and to Canada has been maintained. One point of this comparison is to show that the Spanish period of Jewish immigration was not directly represented in Canada. Nevertheless the influence of the Spanish Jews, which carried over into the second period, was felt in Canada as well. The German-Polish Jews of the second period, even though they were greatly outnumbered by the Russian-Polish Jews of the third period, continued to play an influential role for many years.

It is noteworthy that the very first Jews to settle in those British colonies which later became Canada came because of their occupational status rather than because they were refugees. This holds true for those who settled in Quebec in the 1760s, in Ontario in the 1830s, in British Columbia in the late 1850s, as well as in Manitoba in the late 1870s.[1]

Aaron Hart, Samuel Jacobs and Samuel Judah, who were among the first Jews to arrive without legal hindrance in Canada, came in the entourage of the British army in about 1760. None of them were army officers, as claimed by family tradition. They were simply provisioners to the military establishment. Aaron Hart, founder of the first Canadian Jewish family, may have been recognized as a civilian commissary officer, but he could never have been a regular army officer without becoming converted. (In fact the only Jew who held a true military rank in Canada at that time was Admiral Sir Alexander Schomberg, a convert who commanded a ship in support of General Wolfe's forces in the battle for Quebec in 1759. Schomberg was later knighted for his services as a naval officer, according to Dr. Jacob Marcus, historian and director of the American Jewish Archives.)

Hart, who settled in Trois Rivières, and other Jews who settled in Montreal during that period, quickly became part of the new English Canadian merchant class. The French seigneurs who remained in Quebec after the conquest, however, could not stand the business competition, and in 1766 they addressed a petition to the British authorities complaining about the

> crowd of people [who] have come in, in the wake of the army . . . as clerks and managers for London merchants . . . people of no birth, without education . . . soldiers demobilized from the French army, barbers, serving men . . . even Jews . . . who have not hesitated to raise themselves above the new subjects. . . .

The beginning of Jewish settlement in Toronto was far more prosaic. Between 1838 and 1846 about a dozen Jews arrived in the city from the U.S., England and Quebec and quietly established themselves in various business occupations. On the west coast the circumstances were more colourful since the first one hundred Jews arrived with the Fraser River gold rush of 1858, and some quickly opened businesses in Victoria. Again there was a pithy comment, this time from an Englishman, Alfred Waddington, himself a recent arrival. "Victoria," he wrote, "was assailed by an indescribable array of Polish Jews, Italian fishermen, French cooks, speculators of every kind. . . ."

There was clearly a historical prejudice about the role of the Jews. It is, therefore, not surprising that the pursuit of peddling by many Jews and the efforts of some to become farmers frequently became the subject of controversy. The prejudice against the stereotype of the Jew was reinforced by the image the Canadian authorities had of their country for several decades after Confederation. As proclaimed in Macdonald's National Policy, Canada was a land of great agricultural opportunity in the West for hard-working farm settlers who would become the purchasers of eastern manufactured products. It was considered, however, that there were virtually no opportunities for immigrants in the cities.

The proposal to send some of the Russian Jewish refugees to Canada in 1882 developed in England, where Sir Alexander Galt, the first Canadian high commissioner to London was trying to promote immigration to the West. Jewish community leaders in Montreal and Toronto had been aware since the previous year of the developing exodus of Russian Jews. In Montreal, for example, the newly established branch of the Anglo-Jewish Association had committed itself "to unite in any movement for material aid which the London Committee of the . . . Association may deem necessary. . . ."

They were not too happy, however, at the idea of having to settle hundreds of their eastern brethren in their own midst. This was not due to a reluctance to help but rather to a fear of having large numbers of poverty-stricken Jews from eastern Europe crowding into Canadian cities. It was a reflection of similar views expressed by American Jewish representatives going back to the 1860s. Nevertheless in the decade before 1882 about four thousand eastern European Jews per year had been reaching the U.S., and of this number about one hundred had been coming to Canada each year.

The thought that several hundred refugees would now arrive in the space of a few weeks aroused a concern which was only eased by the proposal that most of them would be sent to the West to settle on the land. And so it was that, of five hundred immigrants who arrived in Canada during May and early June of 1882, only about 10 percent remained in Montreal, and perhaps 5 percent stayed in Toronto. All the rest were sent on directly to the West.

Winnipeg then had a total population of 8000, including 23 Jews. In late May of 1882 the city was recovering from its first major river flood, and it was just beginning to slip from the heights of a railway land boom. Only in the area of immigration did 1882 turn out to be a boom year for Manitoba; close to 70,000 immigrants entered the province that year, including over 44,000 who arrived in Winnipeg, and among them were 350 Jews.

The promise of land for the Jews did not materialize for almost two years, and the immediate result was that, overnight, Winnipeg became the third largest Jewish community in the country. In this respect it surpassed Victoria, British Columbia, where about 100 Jews had been living since 1858, and Hamilton, Ontario, which had a Jewish population of 175.

Parnosse — Earning a Living

When Sir John A. Macdonald first heard about the plan to send some of the Russian Jewish refugees of 1882 to the Northwest to try homestead farming, he called it the "old Clo' move" and said in a letter to Alexander Galt, "The old Clo' move is a good one — a sprinkling of Jews in the North West would do good. They would at once go in for peddling and politics and be as of much use in the New Country as Cheap Jacks and Chapman." The first of Macdonald's predictions came true almost immediately for the simple reason that the government took two years to make land available for a Jewish settlement. Why is it, however, that Jews are remembered as peddlers and politicians but forgotten as farmers? The Canadian experience may be traced to the main stream of European history.

Jews did not originally become traders because of an inborn ability. They were forced into it by the pressure of events dating back to the seventh century of the Christian era. Many Jews in western Europe had been farmers and landowners during the pre-feudal period when farm labour was done by slaves. Gradually, however, the church invoked a decree barring Jews from owning slaves for longer than three months and forbidding them from converting slaves to Judaism. (Jews often gave slaves their freedom after they were converted.) As this law became more strictly enforced, it became impossible for many Jews to continue as farmers. Moreover, during the turbulent centuries preceding the rise of feudalism, landowners were obliged to form military defense associations for self-protection. To join such an association it became necessary to take an oath which eventually took the form of a religious ritual. A conscientious Jew could not possibly take such an oath; he was therefore left without protection from roving bandits or predatory neighbours who coveted his land. This ultimately led to the conversion of some Jews, but those who held to their religion were forced out of the landowning class.

As they were driven off the land, many Jews gradually moved into trading and peddling. Some became successful merchants and a few became financiers or entered the learned professions. But many remained peddlers — buyers and sellers of old clothes and other second-hand wares. Eventually they were restricted to this occupation by law in many parts of continental Europe, and it was thus that Jews acquired "a preternatural acumen" for trading, as historian Cecil Roth describes it.

In the eighteenth century many poverty-stricken Jews began to reach England. They had no craft skills, and in London they were barred from entering established branches of the retail trade. Once again they turned to the second-hand business, and it was thus that the picture of the ubiquitous Jewish peddler, the old Clo' man, emerged. This was the image in the mind of Sir John A. Macdonald when he made his prediction. Those who came from eastern Europe did have other skills and abilities, however, as events soon demonstrated.

In the spring of 1882, after the first 19 Jewish immigrants arrived, a telegram was sent to Toronto asking that the rest be kept there until better arrangements could be made for them. That telegram crossed one from Toronto advising that another 247 Russian Jews were already en route and that government authorities would receive official instructions and advice concerning the immigrants. Whatever that advice was it did not include the promised arrangement for land. Immigrants were hard put to find any kind of work. Some of them helped to lay track for the Canadian Pacific Railway which was moving west to Medicine Hat that summer.

From 1882 to 1883 the number of Jewish peddlers among the permanent residents of Winnipeg recorded in *Henderson's Directory* doubled from four to eight. The latter figure represented about one out of five of the total number of Jews listed in the directory. But of course there is no way of knowing how many unrecorded Jewish peddlers were travelling about in the countryside. Most of the Jews who settled in Winnipeg before 1882 were established in business pursuits such as merchant tailors, dry goods and grocery retailers, cigar storekeepers, and there was one real estate agent. After 1882 their occupations became more varied and included an upholsterer, a capmaker, a watchmaker, an expressman, and carpenters, bricklayers, clerks and tailors — in addition to peddlers and storekeepers.[2]

It took Sir Alexander Galt two years to obtain land for the Jewish immigrants of 1882. By this time only twenty-eight families were still prepared to try their hand at homesteading at the Moosomin site assigned to them, which had become known as New Jerusalem. Inexperience, bad advice, poor management and three years of adverse growing conditions combined to undermine this first farming effort. In 1888 Galt declared the effort a failure and complained that the Jews had sold their crops and cattle and turned to "their natural (!) vocation of peddling."

It is significant, however, that while New Jerusalem was failing, a second group of Jews began farming in 1888 at Wapella. The Weidmans, Lechtziers, Norovlanskys and Gelgerins at Moosomin failed in spite of the help of Galt and the Mansion House Committee in London (named for the town hall where the Lord Mayor of London had convened a meeting in aid of the Russian Jews). At Wapella, however, the Heppners, Barishes and

Jacobsons, most of whom started without direct help, were able to make a go of it. They established a Jewish farm settlement that lasted for more than sixty years, with one family still on the land after eighty-five years.

Between 1890 and 1910 several additional farm settlements of some significance were established in the West, mostly with the help of the Jewish Colonization Association which was founded in 1891 simultaneously in London and Paris. They included Hirsch, Lipton, Sonnenfeld-Hoffer and Edenbridge in Saskatchewan, Bender Hamlet in Manitoba and Rumsey Trochu in Alberta. The Saskatchewan colonies proved to be the most successful; they lasted for fifty years or longer. Not one of these colonies ever had more than fifty families, and the total number of Jewish farmers in western Canada never exceeded 572. In all of Canada the highest count for the Jewish farm population was 2,568, reached in 1921. By 1931 this dropped to 2,188, of which 1,624 were in western Canada.

These figures are low when one considers that at one time there had been talk of settling as many as ten thousand Jewish people on the land in western Canada. Discussions were started with the government in Ottawa during 1891-92 for the founding of a new Jewish colony in the West, which eventually became the Hirsch settlement, some twenty miles east of Estevan. After a favourable meeting of a Jewish delegation from Montreal with Prime Minister John Abbott and Agriculture Minister Sir John Carling in Ottawa in January 1892, a settlement of two thousand families of ten people was proposed. The government did not object to the numbers but explicitly turned down a request for the allocation of contiguous land for such a settlement. This vital point was later forgotten or ignored by all those who took up the cause of Jewish land settlement.

When Sir Wilfrid Laurier visited London in 1897 for the Diamond Jubilee of Queen Victoria, he was approached by Herman Landau, a London Jewish financier and philanthropist, who reminded him of the promise of his predecessor, Sir John Abbott, for a two-thousand-family settlement. Landau apparently used this opportunity to reinforce his plea with Laurier about the problem of the Jewish Sabbath observance. About ten years later Landau claimed that Laurier had promised to grant a Jewish self-government district in Manitoba where Saturday could be substituted for Sunday. This entire episode involving Herman Landau and Laurier turned out to be an apocryphal tale on the basis of which it was claimed for many years that a "historic opportunity" had been forfeited.

The fact is that in 1901 Laurier agreed to a recommendation by Sir Clifford Sifton, his Minister of the Interior, opposing the establishment of a new farm colony of Romanian Jews. A new settlement was established at Lipton, nonetheless, because by the time Laurier's official communique reached London, the first group of Romanian Jewish settlers was already on the high seas and the authorities reluctantly consented to assist with a limited settlement effort. Moreover in 1907 Laurier told the London *Jewish Chronicle* that his government was opposed to the establishment of separate Jewish colonies, large or small. He also made it clear that he was opposed to local self-government for the Jews or any similar group and stressed that Canada was encouraging no immigrants except "agriculturists, farm labourers and domestic servants. . . ." Ordinary workmen or "mechanics" would have a very difficult time and came at their own risk, he declared.

Despite the best efforts to establish Jews on the land, and in spite of repeated warnings about lack of opportunities in the cities, it was in the cities where most of the Jewish newcomers remained. In Montreal and Toronto those who had no skills and could not find factory work were given small loans to buy peddling licenses and obtain supplies to fill a backpack from which they could begin selling wares door-to-door in the city or along village and country roads. It is told that Jacob Diamond, considered the first permanent Jewish settler in Calgary, arrived in that city in 1888 after peddling his way west from Ontario over a period of several years. (Jacob Diamond was the founder of Calgary's first synagogue, the House of Jacob.) But the "Jew pedlar" in Canada ran into the same kind of prejudices in the late nineteenth and early twentieth century decades as did his predecessors in England a century earlier.

In 1895 the "Jew pedlar" became the subject of debate in the House of Commons in Ottawa when Joseph Martin, a Liberal MP from Winnipeg, accused the government of paying for the transportation of a number of Jews from Chicago to Calgary. They were supposed to come to Canada to take up farms, he said, but instead they "had resumed their occupation of peddling" and some of them soon ended in the Calgary jail. Replying to this harangue, which took up five pages in Hansard, Mr. Daly, the Minister of the Interior, charged that Martin was not really concerned about the number of Jews brought to Calgary because he said, "I am the Jew he is after. . . ." (There were no Jews in Parliament at that time.) Daly also disclosed that only a single Jew had ended in jail, and that had been for an offence against "one of his fellow countrymen" and not against any of the old settlers.

In 1897 the occupations of the Jews of Toronto were discussed in the *Mail and Empire* by a graduate student journalist named W.L. Mackenzie King. Toronto then had an estimated twenty-five hundred Jews of which fifteen hundred were Russian and Polish immigrants. While most Jews in the city were engaged in the mercantile field, King wrote, they "have not attained as yet, positions of much importance." Many were already in the clothing trade while others were in jewellery, hardware and footware and often engaged in manufacturing as well as in retailing. "Almost all the second-hand clothing stores and junk shops in Toronto," totalling fifty-eight, were owned by Jews, King reported. Moreover large numbers of Jewish peddlers were going about the city and out among the farmers in the country. "The quantities of old rubbish they collect is something amazing [and] almost the entire rag and scrap iron trade is carried on by Jews."

Describing the area where the Jewish immigrants lived, King wrote, "York Street is distinctively the 'Petticoat Lane' of Toronto, and the south side of Queen for some few blocks is not very different. . . ."

The problem of employment for newcomers quickly became a regular item on the agenda of Jewish welfare organizations in the major centres. A big increase in immigration, resulting from the effects of the Russo-Japanese war, moved the Baron de Hirsch Institute and the Hebrew Benevolent Society of Montreal to establish a labour bureau. It was reported that work had been obtained in Montreal or other parts of Canada for all who arrived in 1905. Moreover the annual report of the Montreal society for that year dealt with the question of providing employment for all those who wanted to come to Canada and provided a different solution to the one being given by Sir Wilfrid Laurier and his government associates.

The society's report saw Canada as "a large country with unbounded resources and with every facility for those who are able and willing to work to procure a living and to make provision for the future." Moreover it spoke of Montreal as a rapidly developing city "containing manufactures of all kinds, the most important railway works in the country and increasing commercial pursuits." Many Jews did find jobs in factories and various commercial occupations, but those lacking skills or ability, especially during periods when jobs were scarce, continued to turn to the peddler's cart.

The unkempt personality of the Jewish peddler was portrayed in a graphic, though not unsympathetic manner, by J. V. McAree, the well-known Toronto journalist. In an article called "The Jews in Canada" in *Maclean's Magazine,* in 1912, he described

the 'sheeny' you can see . . . frequenting the lanes and uttering raucous cries of 'rax, bones, bottles'. . . . They are usually dressed in clothing that was made for somebody else and are [often] adorned . . . with whiskers that were intended for nobody at all.

He described them out with their pushcarts shortly after daylight and toiling for long hours after other workmen had gone home. "The calves of their legs are familiar with dogs' fangs," McAree wrote, "other parts of their bodies are acquainted with Christian boots, yet . . . how joyfully they toil. . . . Most of them have come to us from Russia where their lives were never safe. . . ."

Though somewhat condescending, McAree disclosed a comprehensive and fairly objective view of the Jews in Canada at that time, explaining their religious background, the difference between rich and poor, why they were primarily urban dwellers and the prejudice against them for crowding into the cities.

A year later the *Canadian Jewish Times* of Montreal, Canada's first Jewish publication, inveighed against the Toronto Jewish peddler and made excuses for discussing the problem, not in Montreal, but in Toronto "because it is located there in all its miserable strength." Toronto was said to have one thousand peddlers in that "degrading" occupation which was virtually equated with begging. This was, of course, in particular reference to the rag peddler, the buyer of old junk. Only a few years earlier it had been considered a step above charity to give a man a loan that would enable him to start on a peddling route selling cheap clothing or other wares. The rag peddler was another matter. The *Times* wrote he had become "so grotesque a figure" that gentile mothers were said to invoke the figure of the Jewish peddler as a bogeyman to quieten their children. The *Times* urged "the leading Jews of Toronto" to do something about the growing number of peddlers in their city who were becoming "a real nuisance . . . [and] bringing the Toronto Jewish name into bad repute."

Montreal probably had as many rag peddlers as Toronto and there they could ply their routes six days a week, including Sunday. Catholic Quebec had adopted an exemption to the federal Lord's Day Act passed in Ottawa in 1906. And across the country, the itinerant or customer peddler, as he became known, played his part in bringing sought after wares and amenities to isolated communities and pioneer settlers.

Peddling to Politics

In 1888, a few years after making his prediction that Jews would go in for peddling and politics, Sir John A. Macdonald was called upon to answer a complaint from Col. Arthur Wellington Hart, grandson of Aaron Hart, that "since the foundation of the Government [presumably referring to Confederation] no Jew has ever had proffered or received an appointment of honour or emolument *(sic)*." Col. Hart also stated that "beyond voting and arguing their respective parties' claims," the Jews had not taken a more active part in politics because they felt themselves labouring under a "proscription." He asserted that prejudice would prevent the election of a Jew.

In response Macdonald claimed to be unaware of any prejudice against the employment of Jews in public service. He offered as proof that the son of a converted Jew was serving in one of the public departments. He also told Hart that a year or two earlier "I got an appointment for one of your race in the Post Office service in Toronto." As for running for public office, Macdonald suggested that the Jews "have taken perhaps a wiser course in avoiding the worries of political life. . . ." It is clear that the candor of his private remarks in his letter to Alexander Galt in 1882 gave way to expediency in his reply to Col. Hart in 1888.

The prejudice was real enough, however, since it could be traced back to the same circumstances that originally drove the Jews off the land in western Europe and restricted many of them in England to the role of the "old Clo' " peddler. Once they began to win emancipation from civil disabilities following the French Revolution, Jews in Europe quickly became active in politics, and the right to run for and to hold political office became the ultimate proof of equality. In England the main problem was the inability of the Jews to take the prescribed oath of office "on the true faith of a Christian." (This barrier was not removed until 1858, when Lionel de Rothschild, who had been elected five times to Parliament, was at last able to swear allegiance on the Old Testament, without using the words he objected to. He then took his seat in the House of Commons for the first time.[3]) In Canada Ezekiel Hart, uncle to Arthur Wellington and son of Aaron Hart, was elected to the Assembly in Lower Canada for Trois Rivières in 1807 and again in 1808 and was twice prevented from keeping his seat because of the oath problem.

In 1831 the Lower Canada Assembly actually passed an act granting Jews the right to hold any office. Although this act, proclaimed in 1832, has been called the Magna Carta for the Jews of Canada, it neglected to make provision for the resolution of the oath problem. The result was that in Montreal in 1833, Benjamin Hart and Moses J. Hayes were informed by government officials that they were still not exempt from the Christian form of oath in seeking to qualify for appointment as justices of the peace. (A bill had just been passed in the British House of Commons granting exemption to Jews on taking the oath but it was defeated in the House of Lords.) In Trois Rivières, however, Samuel Becancour Hart, Benjamin Hart's nephew, was permitted to take the oath according to his conscience by Joseph Badeaux, a French-Canadian oath commissioner, thereby becoming the first Jewish justice of the peace. (Perhaps Badeaux was influenced by the fact that in France Judaism had recently been recognized as a subsidized state religion.)

In June 1837 Arthur Wellington Hart (Sir John A. Macdonald's complainant in 1888), who was Benjamin's son, appealed to London in his father's behalf but was told that changing the oath was up to the province. Nevertheless about six weeks later, at the beginning of August, Benjamin Hart and Moses Hayes received their commissions as magistrates directly from London. This happened on the eve of the Lower Canada Rebellion when it became convenient for the authorities in London to overlook the oath problem in anticipation of a special need for their services.

When Arthur Wellington Hart wrote to the first Prime Minister fifty-one years later there were indeed no Jews in public office in Canada. One had served, however, in the House of Commons in Ottawa (Henry Nathan for Victoria, 1871-74) and Jewish participation in Canadian politics actually began with Col. Hart's grandfather, Aaron. In 1770 Aaron Hart joined with twenty other merchants to petition the king for an elected assembly for the new colony. (Hart had already served as postmaster in Trois Rivières.) In 1796, however, when Aaron's eldest son, Moses, wanted to run for election to the Assembly, his father warned him, "you will be opposed as a Jew." It appears that Moses did not heed his father's advice for he issued an appeal offering himself as a candidate in the election of July 1796, "to the worthy Free Electors of the Borough of William Henry" (Sorel, Quebec). He was not elected, but the very early active interest of Jews in Canadian politics is clearly indicated.[4]

At the time of Confederation there was no apparently significant interest by Canadian Jews in political activity although there was at least one Jewish delegate, Mark Solomon of Toronto, at the Great Reform Convention in Toronto in June 1867, which eventually led to the establishment of the Liberal Party. Perhaps some of the long time Jewish residents were less interested in political activity than the Hart family had been earlier in the nineteenth century. A more basic reason is probably the fact that there was a very strongly entrenched Anglo-Celtic establishment in Ontario. It was almost equally as strong in

Quebec in spite of the minority English position in that province. The Anglo power group and the Roman Catholic hierarchy of that day certainly held a degree of prejudice which would not have made it easy for a Jew to seek elective office.

On the west coast, however, things were different. The pre-Confederation period of the Pacific coast colonies of Vancouver Island and British Columbia (they were not united until 1866) was comparable in some ways to that in Lower Canada a century earlier. The Jews who arrived in Victoria with the new population flow, brought about by the gold discoveries on the Fraser River in 1858, immediately became active in everything from business to politics to the volunteer fire brigade.

In the second election for the Vancouver Island Assembly in 1860, Selim Franklin, an English Jew who was at the time the government auctioneer, was elected as one of the members for Victoria and was a supporter of the administration of Governor James Douglas. Like Ezekiel Hart before him, Franklin ran into trouble over the oath of office. His colleagues challenged the manner in which he took the oath and implied that he had acted in an underhanded way. It turned out to be a futile exercise in bigotry since Chief Justice David Cameron prepared a lengthy report showing that Franklin had the legal right to take the Jewish form of oath. The assembly refused to accept this report and decided that only they could change the oath procedure. They didn't really want to unseat Franklin, however, and the real challenge to his election came from his defeated opponent, Amor De Cosmos, founding editor of the *British Colonist* and leader of the Reform movement that eventually sparked B.C.'s entry into Confederation.

Amor De Cosmos, a Nova Scotian born William Alexander Smith, challenged Franklin's election on the grounds that eighteen or twenty Black immigrants from California had been allowed to vote without being legally entitled to do so. They had voted for the two government candidates, Attorney General George Carey and Franklin in appreciation for having been allowed to settle on Vancouver Island. First Governor Douglas, and later the assembly, rejected De Cosmos's efforts to unseat Franklin. A year later a court of revision declared that the Blacks had voted illegally but the decision came too late for any further action by De Cosmos. Franklin kept his seat but suffered defeat in the next general election. He was then returned in a by-election and remained in the assembly until 1866 when he left the colony. (In spite of this incident De Cosmos was neither anti-Semitic nor anti-Black. He fought for a proper naturalization law which was eventually passed in 1861 enabling the Blacks to become citizens. He also defended the Jews when he thought their rights were threatened.)

Shortly before Selim Franklin's departure, his brother Lumley was elected mayor of Victoria, serving for one year. Lumley Franklin proved more popular than Selim but refused all requests to run for office again. He remained in British Columbia, taking part in the movement for the unity of the two colonies as well as in the pro-Confederation movement, until his death in 1873. Most of the other Jews who were active in the politics of the day appear to have been identified with the movement for annexation to the U.S.

After Confederation a series of firsts for Jews in politics and public life occurred, primarily in western Canada. Henry Nathan began his political career in 1870 as an elected member of the last colonial legislative council in British Columbia and was elected to Parliament from Victoria in 1871. He was to remain in the House of Commons until 1874, a firm supporter of the Macdonald government. In 1880 N.L. Steiner was elected to civic office in Toronto, the first Jew to win office in a major city in post-Confederation Canada. In Vancouver, one year after its incorporation in 1886, two Jews, David and Isaac Oppenheimer, were elected to serve on the city council. Moreover in 1888 David Oppenheimer began a four-year term as mayor of Vancouver and became known as the "father" of that city. Yet when he retired as mayor, Vancouver did not have one hundred Jews.

It appears clear that while Jews in western Canada were usually able to run for public office and to win elections without regard to their religion, in the older provinces this was not possible, at least beyond the civic level, for the first fifty years after Confederation. In Montreal special efforts were mounted to open the way for a Jew to get into Parliament. A movement started in the Conservative Party to appoint a Jew to the Senate on the claim that according to population Jews were entitled to two seats in the Upper House. In 1917 the name of David S. Friedman, a Canadian-born experienced community leader, was put forward publicly for appointment to the Senate by a Montreal Conservative party association, but nothing came of it.

At the same time the Liberal Party, then out of office, was persuaded that a constituency on Montreal Island should be recognized as a Jewish seat. This proposal met with the approval of the parliamentary committee then considering the redistribution of seats and thus the Cartier constituency was established. It had a heavy concentration of Jews though they were by no means a majority. Samuel W. Jacobs, a Canadian-born lawyer of well-deserved repute, won the seat for the Liberals in 1917. He was unopposed by the union government of Sir Robert Borden although there were two other candidates. Jacobs sat in the House of Commons with distinction until his death in 1938. It is claimed he was passed over for a Cabinet post by Mackenzie King because of continued opposition to the idea of a Jew in the Cabinet.

In 1918 Peter Bercovitch, also a Liberal, was the first Jew elected to the Quebec assembly. Representing St. Louis, a district corresponding approximately to the federal Cartier riding, Bercovitch carried to the provincial level the idea of a Jewish member for a Jewish seat. This approach appears to have been taken in Toronto when Ephraim Singer, a Conservative, was elected to the Ontario legislature in 1929 for St. Andrew, a riding with a concentrated Jewish population. A year later Samuel Factor, a Liberal, was elected MP for Toronto Spadina, which covered the same neighbourhood at the federal level.

By this time Manitoba had gone further than any other province in electing to office Jews representing different political parties. In 1926, A.A. Heaps was elected to the House of Commons, as a member of the Independent Labour Party (later CCF) from North Winnipeg, and in 1927 William V. Tobias was elected to the provincial parliament as a Conservative. Although Winnipeg North had the largest concentration of Jews in the city, the number was always much smaller than the comparable neighbourhoods in Montreal and Toronto. Winnipeg North rather became one of the first two districts in Canada with a Labour-CCF-NDP tradition and, at the provincial level an area from which Ukrainians, Poles and Jews eventually came to be represented in the Manitoba legislature.[5]

In Ontario the eastern pattern of electing Jews to the federal and provincial parliaments from Jewish neighbourhood districts was broken with the election of David Croll to the legislature from the Windsor area in 1934. Croll had served as mayor of Windsor, a city of over one hundred thousand inhabitants, less than twenty-five hundred of which were Jews. When he entered the Ontario legislature he became the first Jew appointed to the Cabinet of any provincial government in Canada. After the Second World War, Croll succeeded Sam Factor as MP for Spadina and eventually became the first Jew named to the Senate. In Croll's case it was also claimed that, like Samuel W. Jacobs, he was by-passed for appointment to the federal Cabinet.

During the first century of Confederation eleven Jews had held seats in the House of Commons, six of them from the Cartier riding in Montreal. In 1968 when the Cartier constituency was eliminated in redistribution, Montreal did not return a single Jewish member in the general election of that year. But a total of eight Jews were elected to Parliament, including four from predominantly non-Jewish areas in Toronto. The others were from Windsor, Galt, Winnipeg North and Newfoundland. Among them were four Liberals, two NDPers and one Conservative.

In Manitoba the Conservative and Liberal parties in opposition have both been led by Jews in recent years while the NDP government had three Jewish Cabinet ministers[6]. I.H. Asper resigned the Liberal leadership in early 1975 and Sidney J. Spivak was defeated in December, 1975, in his bid to remain as head of the Manitoba Conservative Party and leader of the Opposition. And in 1976 Dave Barrett, the first NDP premier of British Columbia and the first Jew to head a government in Canada, lost his bid for re-election, including his own seat[7]. Ontario now has Stephen Lewis, a Jew, as leader of the NDP official Opposition but this did not stop the Ontario Liberals from repeating the Manitoba experience, of electing another Jew, Dr. Stuart Smith, as their new leader.

After the 1968 election, Herb Gray, the member for Windsor, became the first Jew named to the federal Cabinet. After the 1974 election Prime Minister Trudeau returned Gray to the back benches and brought another Jew, Barney Danson, into the Cabinet. There has been much speculation as to why Gray was dropped and it has become apparent that his voice in Cabinet must have often sounded a discordant note in spite of the fact that he was a public model of Cabinet solidarity. Outside of the Cabinet he has begun to sound more and more like the late Sam Jacobs, the first Jewish member for Cartier, who gained a wide reputation for outspokeness, even at the expense of his party leader.

Synagogue Development

In September 1882 Jewish holy day services were conducted in two locations in Manitoba as a result of the arrival of the three hundred and fifty immigrants earlier in the year. In Winnipeg Rosh Hashanah and Yom Kippur services were held in public for the first time in 1880, at the Orange Hall. The following year the services took place in the Odd Fellows Hall. With the arrival of the 1882 newcomers, larger quarters were needed and the services were moved to the Wesley Hall. About two hundred and fifty people attended the observances in the city that year including some of the men who returned to Winnipeg for the holy days from their jobs with the CPR construction crew.

The CPR had in fact provided a tent for their Jewish workers where they were able to conduct the weekly Sabbath ritual. Some of these men preferred to conduct their own holy day services in the tent and these took place at a railway station forty miles from Winnipeg. This group, numbering about thirty, collected $100 among themselves to send for a Sefer Torah (a scroll containing the Pentateuch, the five books of Moses) and a shofar ("ram's horn"). They observed the holy day "fully and completely," one of their members reported, praying and reading from the Torah. Some local residents watched with wonder and admiration and were said to have commented, "Look! Though far removed from their homes and their people they nevertheless make every effort to worship in the manner known to them."

When these early holy day services took place in Manitoba there were already five established synagogues in other parts of Canada, two in Montreal, and one each in Toronto, Hamilton and Victoria. A third congregation was founded in Montreal in 1882 and the following year Toronto's second synagogue was opened. The Jews of Manitoba conducted simultaneous holy day services in two locations much sooner than early arrivals in any other part of the country and thereby demonstrated the immediate prospect for two congregations.

The first Jewish congregation in Canada had been established in Montreal in 1768, in temporary quarters on St. James Street. Regular services were not inaugurated until the first synagogue building was erected at the corner of St. James and Notre Dame streets in 1777. The congregation was called Shearith Israel ("remnant of Israel"), the Corporation of Spanish and Portuguese Jews, later referred to as the Spanish and Portuguese Synagogue.

All Jewish congregations were Orthodox in those days. But there were two distinctive ritual traditions, the Sephardic customs followed by the descendants of Spanish Jewry who had spread throughout western Europe, and the Ashkenazic practice followed by the early Jews of Germany whose descendants were dispersed through eastern Europe. The Montreal congregation adopted the Sephardic ritual and claimed to be descended from Spanish Jews. Available evidence disputes this since the migration of Spanish Jews to America ended some thirty-five years before the first Jews took up permanent residence in Canada.[8] Nevertheless the Sephardic customs were more highly regarded by most Jews in America until well into the nineteenth century, and the Jews of Montreal were following the example of their co-religionists in New York with whom many of them shared a close kinship.

Wherever a Jewish congregation was started, a cemetery was invariably established even before the synagogue was built. In Montreal the first Jewish burial ground was purchased in 1775 in the vicinity of what later became Dominion Square. In the spring of 1779 the Jews of Montreal were called together to consider a request to bury an uncircumcised child, the son of Ezekiel Solomons. The congregation decided that there were extenuating circumstances on this occasion and approved the burial. It was unanimously agreed, however, that "no Man or Boy whomsoever shall be after Sixty days from this Date be buried in the Burying place of this Congregation unless Circumcised."

By 1846 there were a growing number of Jews in Montreal who wanted to worship according to the Ashkenazic ritual and some twenty-five of them gathered together that year to establish the English, German and Polish congregation. It took this congregation fourteen years until it was able to build its own synagogue which took the name Shaar Hashomayim ("gates of heaven"). This congregation eventually surpassed the Spanish and Portuguese congregation in size and influence, and during the first half of the twentieth century it became the largest Jewish congregation in Canada.

In Toronto the first authentic evidence of organized Jewish community life was the registration in 1849 of a deed for a piece of land on Pape Avenue purchased for a burial ground by Judah G. Joseph and Abraham Nordheimer, as trustees of the Toronto Hebrew congregation. (Nordheimer was one of the founders of the piano and music house of that name which flourished in Toronto for many years.) Establishment of a permanent congregation, however, did not take place until 1856 when the Sons of Israel was organized. A room was rented for a place of worship over Mr. Coombes's drug store at the corner of Yonge and Richmond streets. By 1869 the congregation became known as the Holy Blossom Hebrew congregation and its by-laws specified that it was to follow Orthodox principles and the Polish form of prayer. The latter implied the Ashkenazic ritual.

Toronto's Holy Blossom Temple has been well known for many years as a Reform synagogue but it was not the first Reform congregation in Canada. The Anshe Sholom ("men of peace") founded in Hamilton in 1863 as an Orthodox congregation began to move toward Reform in 1871 under the leadership of Edmund Scheuer, a Franco-German Jew who came from Lorraine. (Scheuer later played a similar role at Holy Blossom in Toronto.) In 1882 when the Hamilton congregation built its own synagogue it became the first officially established Reform temple in Canada. That same year in Montreal seven men gathered together for the explicit purpose of forming a Reform congregation. The name Temple Emanu-El was chosen and the first services were at the High Holy Days that fall, but Montreal's third congregation did not acquire its own synagogue building until ten years later.

The move to Reform by the Holy Blossom congregation in Toronto was much more gradual and in some ways it was concerned with granting women a greater measure of recognition in the synagogue. It had long been the custom in Orthodox synagogues for women to sit separately from men. Where there was no women's balcony, an ultra-Orthodox congregation would erect a curtain or partition to divide the men and women. When such a screen was erected at Holy Blossom in 1868 the women began an immediate revolt and threatened not to attend services. Before very long the screen was removed.

Music was taboo in Orthodox synagogues in the nineteenth century, except for the chanting of the cantor and the occasional singing of a boys choir. Musical instruments were completely barred. In 1873, a few years after Holy Blossom moved into its first synagogue building, Mrs. Rebecca Lyon Morris won permission from the board to form an unaccompanied ladies choir to sing occasionally at services. Some fifteen years later Edmund Scheuer, who had moved to Toronto, proposed that the choir be asked to sing at the Rosh Hashanah services and he won approval of the board by a vote of seventeen to thirteen. This indicated how closely the lines were drawn, and while the move for Reform was gaining strength it continued to be a very gradual process. When an organ was brought into the synagogue for the first time, the cantor resigned though the rabbi found the musical instrument acceptable. On one occasion three members of the congregation carried the organ out of the synagogue and left it in the yard. When the board voted to put it back, they resigned and joined Toronto's second congregation, Goel Tzedec, which had been formed in 1883.

It was not until 1920 when the Hebrew Union College, the Reform seminary in Cincinnati, was asked to suggest a new rabbi that Holy Blossom became officially a Reform synagogue. The change had taken close to fifty years from the time a female choir was first organized. The process also represented a struggle between Jews from Germany where the Reform movement was started in the first half of the nineteenth century and Jews from eastern Poland and Russia where Orthodoxy always prevailed. The same contending elements were to be found in the Jewish communities of Victoria, Winnipeg and Vancouver between 1860 and 1900, and there were similar struggles in the latter two cities though with different results.

In the fall of 1858 the Jews of Victoria gathered in a private home for the holy day services and in May of the following year they met to make plans for the establishment of a cemetery. That cemetery continues to serve the Jewish community of Victoria to this day. In August 1862, twenty Victoria Jews became charter members of Congregation Emanu-El, the fourth in Canada. They immediately launched a campaign for funds for a synagogue building and received contributions from non-Jews as well as Jews. They raised some $4,900 toward the total cost of $9,855, including the land.

On 2 June 1863 the cornerstone was laid for the synagogue at a gala ceremonial event which might, in fact, be called the first multi-cultural program in the West, if not in all Canada. It began with a parade to the synagogue site led by the navy band from H.M.S. *Topaz* at Esquimalt and was followed by members of the Germania Zingverein ("singing club"), the St. Andrew's Society, the French Benevolent Society and two Masonic lodges in full regalia. The actual ceremony was somewhat unusual since it involved the laying of two cornerstones, one by Robert Burnaby, grandmaster of the Masons, and a second by David Shirpser, first president of the congregation. Some congregation members who were Masons persuaded the others that the chief of the Masonic order should be given the cornerstone honour. Later, however, some of the more Orthodox members objected and it was then decided to provide for a second cornerstone. A benediction prayer was read by David Cameron, who was chief justice of Vancouver Island and a Presbyterian Scot.

The Masonic members of the Victoria congregation, together with some others, represented a Reform element, but the Emanu-El Synagogue never considered itself more than semi-Reform. In fact the congregation reported hiring a shochet even before the synagogue was built for those members who wished to observe the dietary laws of Judaism. It was more likely the first Conservative congregation in British North America and claimed "nearly 65" members in its first year.

In Winnipeg, where the Jewish population jumped from twenty-one to three hundred or more by 1883, an attempt was made that year to establish one congregation. The earlier residents who favoured Reform, however, could not come to an understanding with the newcomer majority who affirmed their Orthodoxy. For several years there were two congregations, Beth El (Reform) and Sons of Israel (Orthodox). In 1887 a Manitoba *Free Press* survey of Winnipeg churches found "three congregations of the Hebrew faith" but no synagogue. The lack of a synagogue was correctly attributed to the absence of unity, and the writer commented,

outsiders are apt to underestimate the work accomplished . . . owing to divisions which exist. . . . United the Hebrews would form a Congregation of very respectable numbers and they would soon possess a building creditable alike to themselves and the city.

It took two more years for the Winnipeg Jewish community to achieve a sufficient measure of unity for the building of the first synagogue, Shaarey Zedek ("gates of justice"). The cornerstone was laid in September 1889, and for the second time a principal participant in the ceremomy was the grandmaster of a Masonic lodge, the Rev. Cannon James Dallas O'Meara. It was almost certainly the very first occasion on which a woman, young Bessie Finkelstein, participated in such a ceremony. She made a little speech and presented the trowel to Cannon O'Meara.

It was an Orthodox congregation but the unity did not last long. Apparently there were some east Europeans who preferred the Sephardic ritual rather than the Ashkenazic form of worship. They began to hold a separate service at the Shaarey Zedek Synagogue but before long they broke away, and by 1893 they had built Winnipeg's second synagogue. This became known in Yiddish as the Sefardishe Shul but its official name was Rosh Pina ("the cornerstone").

The very first Jewish religious services in the city of Vancouver are said to have taken place in 1887 in the home or store of Zebulon Franks, a Russian-born Orthodox Jew who arrived in the city earlier that year from Winnipeg. (A photograph of the Franks' store on Water Street was the model for William Kurelek's general store painting. The Franks family later established Y. Franks Ltd., an appliance store which was well known in Vancouver for many years. Zebulon Franks also made arrangements to bring in kosher meat from Seattle.) It was not until the fall of 1892, the year after David Oppenheimer completed his term as mayor, that the first High Holy Day services were held in a public place, at the Knights of Pythias Hall on Cordova Street. The Yom Kippur evening service was reported in the Vancouver *Daily World*, 1 October 1892, under the heading "God's Peculiar People." The reporter wrote,

Not until the first star appears in the sky this evening will any devout Jew in the city or for that matter in the whole world have tasted a morsel of food or drank a drop of water for the space of 24 hours. With God's peculiar people in every land under the heavens, today is a day of solemn fasting, serious reflection, devout repentance for past sins and imploration *(sic)* to have them forgiven, in fact it is the old Mosaic Day of Atonement, and as such is solemnly observed with faces turned eastward.

According to the Vancouver *World* the congregation was known as the Agudace Achim Society (literally, "the organization of brothers") and Rabbi S.S. Hyams of Victoria gave the sermon, "a practical address . . . delivered in the English language, interlarded at frequent intervals with Hebrew quotations."

Another 1887 arrival in Vancouver was Samuel Gintzburger, Swiss-born and German educated, who leaned to Reform. Gintzburger played a leading role in pioneer Jewish community endeavors with the result that by 1894 there were two functioning congregations, the Orthodox Sons of Israel under Franks' leadership and the semi-Reform Temple Emanu-El, headed by Gintzburger. It took about twenty years until the two groups were able to unite to build Vancouver's first synagogue. There, too, a second congregation was started soon after the Orthodox Schara Tzedeck Synagogue opened.

If the development of early Jewish congregations and synagogues in Canada appears to have been uncoordinated it may be attributed to the fact that while the Jewish religion is monotheistic it is not monolithic. Moreover Judaism has not had a priestly hierarchy since the destruction of the Second Temple in 70 C.E. ("common era"). The descendants of Aaron were the Cohanim, or priests, in the days of the Temple, and the descendants of the tribe of Levi were the Levites, a second rank of Temple functionaries. Jews with the surname Cohen and Levy and various derivations of those names are recognized as descendants of the priests or Levites of ancient times. They are called upon to observe certain special customs and privileges in the synagogue. (The priestly descendants in particular, if they are observant Orthodox Jews, must abide by certain special religious laws including one governing the choice of a wife.)

The rabbi, who is the spiritual leader of the congregation or synagogue in modern times, need not be a Cohen or a Levy. In fact *rabbi* is a Hebrew word meaning teacher and is traced back to Moses, who has been referred to in every generation as Mosheh Rabbenu, "our teacher Moses." Most contemporary rabbis are duly ordained by the rabbinical college or seminary where they completed their studies. However, a congregation may name as its spiritual leader or rabbi anyone who is considered qualified to fulfil the required functions. Orthodox congregations in smaller communities have sometimes conferred the title rabbi on a man originally hired as cantor (chazzan or "prayer leader") and shochet ("ritual slaughterer"). Usually this would only occur if the man has demonstrated his ability as a teacher and interpreter of Jewish religious law. One example in Canadian experience is that of Marcus Berner.

Marcus Berner, born in 1865, trained as a cantor and shochet in Lithuania. He served with a congregation in England and then came to Canada in 1899 to become a homestead farmer at Hirsch, Saskatchewan. After thirty-two years of fulfilling simultaneous duties as a farmer and a religious functionary, he moved to Victoria where he was appointed rabbi of Congregation Emanu-El and served there for the rest of his years.

Just as rabbi means teacher, the synagogue, which originally meant assembly or congregation (Hebrew: "Bet Haknesset"), became better known over the centuries as Bet Hamidrash, a house of study as well as prayer. In Canada this was carried over by east European Jews who called the synagogue the shul or sheel which is Yiddish for school. Over the centuries the synagogue kept the Jews together, not only as the place for community assembly, prayer and study but also as the house of judgment and the centre of charity. Significantly, the synagogue, from its inception twenty-five hundred years ago, introduced the idea that each worshipper, without priestly intervention, could achieve personal communion with God. Because of this concept of a direct relationship between man and God, the devout individual Jew could fulfil his personal religious obligations (for example, prescribed daily prayers) right in his own home, or whatever place he happened to be if travelling.

Wherever Jews lived, once they had sufficient numbers to form a minyan ("prayer quorum of ten men") it was considered an obligation to gather together to organize a congregation and establish a synagogue, not only for worship, but to fulfil all the aforementioned objectives which constitute the essential elements of a community. Through the centuries the synagogue became the centre for the organization of the Jews as a community within the larger community of Gentiles ("non-Jews"). The Jewish community organization based on the synagogue, became known as the kehillah or kahal.

In eastern Europe, where most Canadian Jews or their forebears originated, the kehillah became a form of self-government which was enforced upon the Jews by the kings of Poland for over two hundred years and later by the Russian czar until the mid-nineteenth century. In spite of many adverse features imposed by the authorities when it was a compulsory form of self-rule, the Jews favoured the kehillah plan of community organization as a means of maintaining religious continuity.

After they began coming to Canada in large numbers in 1882, there were some Jews who felt that the kehillah could be re-introduced on a voluntary basis. However, the millennia-long absence of an established religious hierarchy, combined with the vastly expanded opportunities of living in a free country, encouraged the tendency toward greater variation in congregational style and religious practice. Nevertheless, in the total of approximately 200 Jewish congregations now established in Canada (for a population of about two hundred and eighty thousand, some 150 to 175 are officially Orthodox, about 25 are Conservative and possibly 8 or 9 are Reform.

Almost every one of the Conservative and Reform congregations is served by a rabbi, but among the Orthodox synagogues only about eighty to eighty-five of the larger ones have rabbis. The presence or absence of a rabbi depends, of course, on the size and financial means of the congregation. There is also a tradition in Judaism by which any group of ten men who form a permanent minyan, as the nucleus of a congregation, should be able to find one of their number who can act as baal tefillah, or prayer leader. Thus a rabbi is not always an absolute necessity.

As the twentieth century began and Jewish immigration increased, synagogues began to proliferate, particularly in larger centres such as Montreal or Toronto. Some congregations were formed by groups of men who came from the same old-country town, or country, like the Anshei Ozeroff or Anshei Ukraine in Montreal, the Anshei Minsk, or the Hebrew Men of England Synagogue in Toronto (anshei means "men of"). Occasionally a synagogue became known by the trade of most of its members and in the 1920s, for example, there were synagogues in Winnipeg known as the Peddlerishe Shul and the Butcher's Shul.

The reader may have observed by now that Orthodox and Reform congregations have been mentioned frequently in discussing the growth of synagogues in Canada but suddenly a third denomination has appeared, the Conservative congregation. Before placing the Conservative synagogue into its Canadian context it would be well to endeavour to define a little more precisely the three major denominations of contemporary Judaism.

Prior to the nineteenth century all Jews were orthodox (small o) although the term itself was completely unknown. There were differences of course as reflected in the Ashkenazic and Sephardic traditions, based originally on geographic origin and later on social predilection. It was primarily a question of minhag ("custom"). Minhag Ashkenaz differed from Minhag Sefard in style of liturgy, ritual and ceremonies much more than

in substance. The two best examples are in the difference of Hebrew pronunciation and the music of the synagogue, even though the latter was limited to the chanting and singing of the chazan ("cantor") and the male choir.

The Chasidic movement which rose in eastern Europe in the first half of the eighteenth century, has been simplistically described as "a sect of Jewish mystics." Chasidism, however, was really a movement to save the Jews from their depressed state following a period of intense persecution in Poland. It taught that all men were equal before God and that the poor and unlearned man could achieve communion with God through piety just as easily as the scholar. The Chasidim ("the pious ones") proclaimed joyous abandonment to prayer and spirituality. Their critics, the Misnagdim (literally, "opponents") emphasized the rationalism of the Talmud (the rabbinic writings forming the basis of Jewish religious authority).

When the political emancipation of the Jews began in western Europe in the late eighteenth century as part of the general enlightenment that came in the wake of the industrial revolution, it also spurred a Jewish enlightenment movement known as the Haskalah. The ideas which led to the development of Reform Judaism came from the advocates of Haskalah. They felt that the barriers keeping Jews and Christians apart must be removed, urged the Jews to abandon religious-cultural exclusivism and to cease being "God's peculiar people." Obviously this produced a sharp reaction among the adherents of traditional Talmudic Judaism.

The Reform movement also became known as Liberal or Progressive Judaism. When the first Reform temple was opened in 1818 in Hamburg, Germany, men and women sat together in family pews, the men went bareheaded into the synagogue, and the custom of uninhibited praying aloud, spread by the Chasidic movement, was discarded. In daily morning prayers the use of tefillin ("phylacteries") was abolished. In the temple hymns were sung in German to organ accompaniment played by a Christian and the sermon was delivered in German. In a word,

Christian style and decorum was brought into the synagogue. Eventually kashrut, the dietary law separating meat and milk and governing the slaughter of animals and the cooking of meat, was declared obsolete.

All at once the vast majority of traditional Jewry discovered that they were Orthodox. In opposition to the Reform movement a school of modern Orthodoxy developed within a few years, also based in Germany. While agreeing to the need for harmony between Judaism and science, the teachings of the Torah and recognized institutions of Judaism such as the Shulchan Aruch ("the code of religious law") were reaffirmed as an absolute guide even for enlightened Jews seeking modernity. Orthodox adherents were enjoined to maintain all the rules and customs being abandoned by the Reform group. The latter also rejected the Sabbath ban against lighting a fire or riding in any kind of vehicle. Some modification in long-standing customs did occur among the modern Orthodox followers, for example, the men gave up the practice of wearing beards and earlocks or flowing sideburns, married women stopped wearing the sheitel ("wig") which had been the custom since the Middle Ages. Orthodoxy itself now split into three groups with ultra-Orthodox fundamentalists on one side of the neo-Orthodox and the Chasidim as a sectarian other-worldly group on the other.

The position of Reform at the very opposite pole of Orthodoxy, in any of its variations, is confirmed by the fact that modern Orthodoxy asserted Torah precepts to be immutable while Reform Judaism denied that the Torah was divinely revealed truth. By the middle of the nineteenth century, however, there was a movement back from Reform proclaimed as "positive historical Judaism" and defined as "Reform tempered by Conservatism." Thus Conservative Judaism came to take up the ground between modern Orthodoxy and liberal Reform Judaism.

In applying this approach Conservative Judaism accepted mandatory submission to the authority of Biblical principles and rabbinic law but adherence depended on whether rulings based on the religious code responded to the contemporary requirements of Jewish life. For example the Conservative approach rejected the Orthodox view that the ban on making a fire or doing any kind of work on the Sabbath extends to pressing a button to turn on a light or to use an elevator. Conservative synagogues also allowed mixed seating. Kashrut was recognized as obligatory but in a less rigid form; for example, where Orthodox adherents may eat no food whatsoever in a home or restaurant that is not strictly kosher, Conservative followers may eat fish or dairy dishes where kosher meat is unavailable.

It has already been explained that Orthodoxy and Reform were both represented in the formation of congregations and the establishment of synagogues in Canada before 1900. The continuing competition between Orthodox and Reform elements in certain congregations led to the entry of Conservatism as a compromise approach. The Shaar Hashomayim Synagogue in Montreal became Conservative soon after the turn of the century and, before many years had passed, Toronto's second synagogue, Goel Tzedec, became Conservative. In Winnipeg the conflict between the various elements that built the first synagogue, Shaarey Zedek, resulted in a number of splits over several decades, but finally a breakaway Reform group returned to the fold in 1913 and the congregation became Conservative. In Vancouver the early Reform congregation suspended its activities to support the building of the first synagogue in 1918 which was Orthodox. When the former Reform element eventually came together again they established a Conservative congregation, Beth Israel.

In certain European countries the absence of an established religious hierarchy was countered by the appointment of a chief rabbi. In France the office of grand rabbin was created by government regulation under Napoleon. In Britain the position of chief rabbi came about informally. In Israel, where it has become best known, the office of chief rabbi was established by a ruling of the British Mandatory regime.

The position of chief rabbi has never been officially recognized in Canada. Certain individual rabbis have come into prominence by virtue of their personal scholarship and leadership. Probably the most distinguished rabbi ever to serve in Canada was Dr. Abraham de Sola who served as spiritual leader of the Spanish and Portuguese Synagogue of Montreal from 1847 to his death in 1882. One year after he arrived in Montreal he was named professor of Hebrew and Oriental literature at McGill University and held that position for the rest of his life. De Sola was an authentic Sephardic Jew, the son of the senior rabbi of London's leading synagogue and grandson of a chief rabbi of Sephardic Jews in Britain.

During the first half of the twentieth century the best known rabbi in eastern Canada and probably throughout the country was Rabbi Dr. Herman Abramowitz, who was the spiritual leader of the Shaar Hashomayim congregation in Montreal from 1903 until his death in 1947. Rabbi Abramowitz not only served his congregation but the community as a whole, and he was a prime mover in local welfare undertakings, such as the Federation of Jewish Philanthropies, as well as in the Zionist Organization and the development of Canadian Jewish Congress. He served on the Canadian Committee of the Jewish Colonization Association and visited the western Jewish farm settlements before the First World War.

In the West Rabbi Israel Kahanovitch was the outstanding religious leader, from his arrival in 1906 to head the House of Jacob, the best known Orthodox synagogue in Winnipeg, until his death in 1945. By virtue of his leadership in religious and communal affairs he was acknowledged as chief rabbi in Winnipeg and throughout the West.

At least half of all observant religious Jews describe themselves as Orthodox to this day. This means that about half the Jews who are synagogue members belong to Orthodox congregations. In the old country every Jew belonged to the synagogue as a matter of course — except in the extreme case of having been excommunicated. People did not become members of the synagogue the way it is done today. Moreover the synagogue is today no longer the one and only Jewish community institution. For observant Orthodox Jews the motivation for belonging to a synagogue is clear. Others may be motivated to retain a sense of religious identity even if they are not strictly observant. In such cases the desire for synagogue affiliation may be no different than it is for Protestant Christians who seek church affiliation.

Even though each synagogue has its own membership group it is still open to the community, and anyone may attend services whether a member or not. Year-round synagogue participation is probably much lower than the 50 percent of the population who may be members. During the holy days of Rosh Hashanah and Yom Kippur, when the motivation is much stronger, participation in services and temporary affiliation by way of seat purchases may rise to 75 or 80 percent of the adult community.

Probably the truest indicator of Jewish religious identity is to be found in the home although this is difficult to measure or assess. Such identification may mean the observance of all traditions and customs prescribed for the home on Sabbath and other festival days, or it may be limited to the display of rarely used candlesticks, a mezuzah on the front door frame, or possibly a shelf of books. (The mezuzah is a container with a parchment scroll of Biblical quotations which has come to be regarded as an amulet to protect the home from outside harm.)

Historically the Sabbath is the most important holy day among the Jews, next to Yom Kippur. There are special services in the synagogue Friday evening and Saturday morning, but the home is the focus of Sabbath observance. While father is still at the synagogue, mother lights the candles to usher in the Sabbath. The table has been set with a white tablecloth and the challah ("Sabbath bread") covered with an embroidered napkin. On arriving home father recites the Kiddush, the prayer of sanctification, which includes the blessing of a glass of wine. This is the ceremonial beginning of the Sabbath meal. The home is thus especially sanctified as the place in which the family gathers for a day of rest and harmony. Marital intercourse on Friday night is recommended by the rabbis. On Saturday evening immediately after sundown, the separation of the Sabbath from the weekdays is marked by the service of Havdallah ("distinction") which includes blessings over the flame of a braided candle, a box of spices and a large glass of wine.

The extent to which these ceremonies are carried out in homes which are not strictly Orthodox is purely a matter of personal choice. Conservative rabbis have always urged Sabbath observance as strongly as their Orthodox confreres and many Reform rabbis are now placing a stronger emphasis on Sabbath rituals. Even in homes without synagogue affiliation, Friday evening is often regarded as the time for a special family meal with or without the ritual ceremonies.

Special home observances are part of Jewish family tradition on the High Holy Days (Rosh Hashanah and Yom Kippur), during the week of thanksgiving (Sukkot), which begins five days after Yom Kippur, and especially on the first two days of Passover. The family gathering at Rosh Hashanah is similar to that of the Sabbath with the additional ceremony of eating a piece of bread or apple dipped in honey accompanied by a prayer for a "sweet year." On Yom Kippur eve the ceremonial family meal must be completed before sundown when the twenty-four hour fast begins. The family gathering is repeated the next day to break the fast after the last prayer has been recited in the synagogue following sundown. During the week of Sukkot, family meals are taken in the sukkah, a temporary shelter made of light wood, tree branches and similar material. This is reminiscent of the temporary dwellings used by the Israelites during their forty years of wandering in the desert and later by Jewish farmers during the harvest season in ancient Palestine.

The most significant family gathering of the entire year is that which takes place around the seder table on the first two nights of Passover. This is because the festival celebrating the liberation from slavery in ancient Egypt has been at the centre of great and sometimes cataclysmic events in world history, from the crucifixion of Christ to the holocaust of World War II. The Last Supper was a Passover supper, from which some of the customs associated with the Christian Easter festival are derived, such as the Easter egg which has derived from the roasted Passover egg on the seder plate.

Accusations levelled at the Jews over Christ's death on the cross were often the cause of attacks against them in Europe at Passover time. One of the most serious attacks on the Jews began on the first night of Passover in 1943 when the Nazi army began the final destruction of the Warsaw Ghetto. This was, of course, part of Hitler's plan for the "final solution" of the Jewish question, arising from his racist philosophy of Aryan superiority. In launching the attack on Passover, the Nazis were also taking advantage of ancient Christian prejudice against the Jews.

In Canada Jews have always celebrated Passover without fear of repression. In renewing family ties at the Seder table Canadian Jews recall the experience of their fathers and grandfathers in Europe as well as of their ancient forebears. A special ritual of remembrance has been added to the Seder ceremonies for the six million Jews who perished at the hands of the Nazis and for the heroes of the ghetto uprisings during World War II. The Passover festival is the outstanding example of how Jewish religious customs and practices are linked from historic to contemporary times.

The same holds true for Chanukah, the Feast of Lights, which is a secondary festival from the religious point of view. Celebrated in December, Chanukah also has historic contemporary significance. It has acquired special importance in many Jewish homes partly because it usually comes at the time of year when most of the community at large celebrates Christmas. In the home Chanukah is especially appealing to the children because of the lighting of candles for eight nights in a special candelabra called the Chanuka Menorah, to commemorate the victory of the Maccabees over the Syrians in 165 B.C.E. ("before the common era"). The candle-lighting ceremony, beginning with one candle and adding another each night, is derived from the legend of a miracle which occurred when the

Maccabees restored the Temple in Jerusalem and a one-day supply of holy oil burned for eight days until a new supply was obtained to keep the eternal lamp burning. There is a special benediction for the candle-lighting ceremony and afterwards parents and other older relatives distribute Chanukah gelt ("money") and other gifts to the children.[9]

What about Jews who don't go to the synagogue and don't practice religious rites? There have always been among the Jews those who were careless in observing religious laws, skeptics who challenged cherished Jewish beliefs, scoffers, free-thinkers and unbelievers, and even some who called themselves agnostics or atheists. Any one of these who has ceased to believe in some or all of the basic principles of Judaism but has not gone over to another religion is known as an apikoros or epikoros after the Greek philosopher Epicurus. The Greek origin was forgotten in the course of time, and the term in Yiddish was applied to anyone who was considered a heretic or free-thinker. By the early 1900s Canada was beginning to acquire some Jews who were knowledgeable in the Torah and Jewish religious traditions but who had rejected much of it and sometimes all of it. Orthodox Jews decried them as apikorsim, or unbelievers, yet many of them made a positive contribution to Jewish life, particularly in the field of education. It would not do, however, to let this episode of Jewish life in Canada come in ahead of its allotted place. It is therefore time to turn back to 1882 and the beginnings of organized Jewish education in Canada.

Education

Concern for education was manifest from the very first arrival of Jews in Canada. In the late 1700s, some parents sent their children to New York or Philadelphia for Jewish schooling if they could not do the teaching themselves. After the establishment of a synagogue, the Jewish school was the second permanent institution to be inaugurated.

Within a few months after the arrival of the Russian Jewish immigrants in Winnipeg in 1882, one of them expressed embarrassment over the inability to secure teachers to instruct the children "in the knowledge of our tradition." He stated, "We are badly in need of a school for them."

While the Winnipeg immigrants were worrying about how to begin the education of their children, the Montreal Jewish community was confronted with the first of many crisis situations over their relationship to the "common" school system of the province of Quebec which took the place of public schools in other provinces.

During the early 1800s religious education had been carried on intermittently at the Spanish and Portuguese Synagogue in Montreal. The establishment of the first permanent school was undertaken by Rabbi Abraham de Sola, who became the spiritual leader in 1847. Under Rabbi de Sola's leadership the school developed from a Sunday school, giving Hebrew and religious instruction, to a day school where other subjects were also taught. When the German and Polish congregation, Shaar Hashomayim, built their first synagogue in 1860 a religious school was soon opened there as well.

In 1874 the new congregation, which was growing in strength, proposed the establishment of a community day school to include secular as well as religious subjects and to be undertaken as a cooperative venture by the two synagogues. A joint committee was named to consider the matter and recommended that a Jewish free school should indeed be established run by a six-member board of commissioners with three from each congregation. The committee made recommendations on the curriculum, the age group to be taught, the appointment and payment of teachers and the estimated cost of the school to be shared by the two congregations. The joint committee appears to have agreed unanimously on all matters except one. It was proposed that the Hebrew language be taught "according to the German pronunciation only," thus deferring to the Ashkenazic minhag or custom.

David A. Ansell, one of the most active members of the Jewish community during the second half of the nineteenth century, was chairman of the joint committee. Because he was a member of the Spanish and Portuguese Synagogue, Ansell reported to his president that he could not accept the proposition that the children be taught "according to the German minhag only. . . . It was an insult to the community I represented," he said, "to ignore entirely the Portuguese minhag" (Sephardic). But, the other synagogue would not sanction any other arrangement, Ansell reported. He therefore recommended that the Portuguese congregation consider "the immediate establishment of a school for ourselves, at which not only our own children, but those of the German-English congregation may attend if they wish[10]."

They undoubtedly knew that, according to Quebec regulations under the BNA Act, a Jewish day school combining secular and religious subjects might qualify for a subsidy through the Protestant school board. Each synagogue soon established its own school and began to share in the school subsidy. The two schools continued to receive grants from the Protestant board until June 1882, when the board withdrew from this arrangement pleading "the diminution of its revenues." To soften the blow the board advised that it was also discontinuing its grant to the St. George's Church School.

In place of the subsidies the board now offered to accept Jewish children into its own schools on the same terms and conditions as Protestant children and stated they would be exempt from scripture lessons and any religious exercises to which their parents objected. They also offered to appoint and pay the salary of a Hebrew teacher nominated by the Jewish congregations and to assign the time and facilities for Hebrew instruction. These proposals were made subject to the condition that school taxes from Jewish properties continue to be paid into the Protestant panel rather than the Roman Catholic or neutral panel.

Although these proposals appeared fairly straightforward at the time, they were complicated by the fact that the two congregations were determined to maintain their own schools. The Spanish and Portuguese congregation actually entered into an arrangement whereby Jewish school taxes were paid to the Catholic panel and the congregational school began to receive funds from the Roman Catholic school board. This continued into the 1890s by which time the Jewish population had risen to such an extent that the Young Men's Hebrew Benevolent Society, which established the Baron de Hirsch Institute, felt compelled to open a community free school for immigrant children, in addition to a sheltering home. By 1892 David Ansell was serving as chairman of the school committee of the Baron de Hirsch Institute and became involved in a dispute with the school board of the Spanish and Portuguese congregation over a share of taxes for the school for immigrant children.

Jewish school taxes eventually went back to the Protestant panel where the problem became aggravated by the continued increase in the number of Jewish students. At one point the Protestant school board complained that the cost of education for Jewish children in its schools was greater than the total of school taxes being paid by Jewish property owners. This particular situation did not last long but the school controversy continued for many years, and it is dealt with here to show how the great concern of the Jews for the education of their children (both secular and religious) became unduly complicated in Quebec because of Section 93 of the BNA Act which guaranteed the education rights of Protestants and Catholics only.

The fathers of Confederation never imagined that Quebec would eventually have other significant minority groups in addition to English-speaking Protestant Christians. Section 93 came to be interpreted in such a way that the granting of minority education rights to Jews could have been an infringement of the entrenched rights of Protestants and Catholics. This view was eventually confirmed by a decision of the Privy Council in London in 1928. That is why, for the purpose of general education, the Jews of Quebec were considered as Protestants in the matter of paying school taxes and sending their children to school.

In 1902 a Jewish student who won a high school scholarship was denied the right to hold it by the Protestant school board of Montreal because his parents were tenants and not property-owning taxpayers. The parents took the school board to court. This was one of a series of legal battles over Jewish school rights carried on in the legislature as well as in the courts. Other issues included the right of Jewish taxpayers to be members of the Protestant school board and the right of Jews to serve as teachers in Protestant schools.

Since the Protestant schools were clearly denominational they also had every right to make Christian religious instruction part of the curriculum. Whenever new regulations were introduced for the acceptance of Jewish children in these schools, as the Protestant board had a right to do, official exemption from religious classes was always included. According to Simon Belkin, who has recorded the school experience in Montreal from the point of view of the immigrant parents, Jewish students were not actually freed from attendance at religious classes until some parents began to send written requests for this exemption. Many parents were unaware that they might do this, while others didn't want to make an issue of it for fear of segregating their children. By the late 1920s however Jewish children were winning and holding scholarships, Jews were beginning to teach in the schools and even the issue of religious exercises faded away. But the major issue of equal rights for Jews in all matters relating to education in Quebec was not fully settled until the period of the "quiet revolution" in the 1960s.

In Ontario the Jews never encountered the same kind of problems in sending their children to the public schools, although there were some religious groups in Toronto who sought to turn the schools into Christian denominational institutions. In 1897 the Anglican church clergy asked the Toronto Public School Board to approve the introduction of a course in religious education, expressing special concern for the poor of St. John's ward where the children were said to be very deficient in their knowledge of religious subjects. Since the Jewish immigrant population was heavily concentrated in this neighbourhood the leaders of the Holy Blossom Synagogue appeared before the board to object to the Anglican request. They said that approval of religious instruction in the schools would "encroach on our rights and liberties" and attack the underlying principle of the public school. The Baptists also objected, calling it a violation of the principle of separation of church and state. On that occasion the school board rejected the Anglican proposal but fifty years later the Ontario government legislated religious studies into the school curriculum.

The 1897 Jewish delegation had told the board that the congregation was conducting Sabbath school classes three times a week because of "the necessity of religious instruction for our children." They suggested that the church might follow their ex-ample by putting more effort into their own Sabbath schools. By the turn of the century Jewish communities in all the larger centres had indeed set an example in establishing their own religious schools, usually in association with synagogues and funded entirely from Jewish community resources.

After 1882 the increase in Jewish immigration began to bring about a change in character as well as a numerical increase in schools for Hebrew and religious education. The nature of these changes is perhaps best exemplified by the Winnipeg experience which was cited fifty years ago in a report on Hebrew and religious instruction in Canada and suggested that other large centres should follow Winnipeg's example (Arthur Daniel Hart, ed., *The Jew in Canada,* Toronto, 1926). The east European immigrants brought with them the old country cheder, the one-room school, sometimes attached to a synagogue but often located in the home of the teacher. A cheder was started by the Winnipeg newcomers in 1884 with twelve students being instructed in the Yiddish language. One year earlier a religious school had been opened by the Beth El congregation teaching the Bible and Jewish history in English to about fifty students. Both schools had their ups and downs as teachers came and went, but the Sabbath or religious school, favoured by those who were already English-speaking, grew stronger after the Shaarey Zedek Synagogue was built.

As the twentieth century began, H.L. Weidman, (one of Alexander Galt's so-called "vagabonds" from the ill-fated Moosomin settlement) who had become a recognized leader of the Shaarey Zedek, came forward with a plan for the establishment of a Talmud Torah school patterned on the community sponsored elementary Hebrew schools in some of the larger east European centres. In America, too, the Talmud Torah was becoming the recognized form of Hebrew free school for the entire community. By 1902 the first Canadian Talmud Torah was opened in Winnipeg in a new building next to the synagogue. It was named the Edward School after the new British monarch. Within four years the growing number of children and differences in curriculum orientation led to the establishment of a second school, the B'nai Zion Hebrew School, associated with a new synagogue of the same name.

The Winnipeg population continued to grow and by 1908 the leaders of both schools agreed to establish a united Hebrew school. The Winnipeg Talmud Torah soon became a reality and had 250 students in 1911. Moreover by 1913 there was a new main school building at Flora and Charles streets which doubled as a community centre. Several branches were established to serve different neighbourhoods but all were operated under the same school board. This united approach to Hebrew education, strengthened after the arrival of Rabbi Kahanovitch, led to the acclaim Winnipeg received in a 1915 New York Yiddish publication for having one of the three top-rated Talmud Torahs in the U.S. and Canada (the other two were in New York and Boston).

The acknowledgement of Winnipeg's example in the Hart publication cited earlier was particularly significant since Montreal had acquired its first Talmud Torah school in 1898. According to Protestant school board records there were some eleven hundred Jewish school age children in Montreal in 1898. For a time the first Talmud Torah was located at a place called Shapiro's Minyan on Cadieux Street. It could hardly have catered to all the children taking Hebrew studies after regular school hours. Many of them were attending the various one-room chedarim that had been started in different neighbourhoods as well as the Baron de Hirsch Institute Hebrew classes and synagogue Sunday schools. In addition some were taught privately at home by visiting melamdim ("itinerant teachers").

In 1917 five independent Talmud Torah Hebrew schools with eight hundred students joined together as the United Talmud Torahs of Montreal. By 1924 there were eight constituent schools, including one yeshiva, with a total of about thirteen hundred students. (A yeshiva is a Hebrew academy devoted to advanced studies in the Talmud and rabbinic literature. It may be a Hebrew secondary school or a school for the training of rabbis and university level studies.) Nevertheless according to the 1926 report on Hebrew and religious education the United Talmud Torahs of Montreal still did not "embrace all places of learning as in Winnipeg."

In Toronto the development of Hebrew education, from the first religious school in 1859 associated with the Sons of Israel (forerunner of Holy Blossom) to the mushrooming of the one-room cheder in the 1890s, was similar to that of Montreal, but the first Talmud Torah Hebrew school was not established there until 1907. By 1926 Toronto had at least seven independent Talmud Torah schools and the move to unite them in a Hebrew education system was just getting underway. Hebrew schools established to this point were conducted after regular school hours. The parochial or day school as it is known today had not yet been started in the Hebrew stream of Jewish education.

Until 1900 Jewish newcomers to Canada from eastern Europe were almost 100 percent Orthodox and Hebrew-education oriented. In Montreal and Toronto the newcomers had to contend with fairly strong Jewish establishment groups many of whom were oriented to Jewish studies in English with supplementary Hebrew. In Winnipeg the pre-1882 arrivals were quickly swamped by the newcomers who by the turn of the century and possibly sooner had themselves become the Jewish establishment. (This is why a united effort for the building of the first synagogue could not be achieved in Winnipeg until 1889, and a second one was quickly established.) Once the east Europeans became strong enough to influence decisively the course of religious development in Winnipeg, it became easier to achieve unity in the building of a Hebrew school system. In Montreal and Toronto the old establishment remained a very strong group for the first two decades of the twentieth century and, while the newcomers quickly gained in strength, the two elements were more evenly balanced for quite a few years. In addition the larger number of newcomers led to greater divergence of views even within the Orthodox element. For these reasons the building of a united Hebrew school system took a longer time in the older centres.

At the turn of the century, as the biggest immigration decade in Canadian history began, the character of the Jewish immigrants became much more varied. Many of these newcomers had been strongly influenced by the socialist-oriented ideologies which had found fertile ground during the turbulent decades of the dying czarist empire. Among the new arrivals were socialists, bundists, territorialists and even anarchists as well as a growing number of labour Zionists. Many of them were questioning the tenets of Orthodox Judaism, the only kind they knew, and a few were agnostics and even atheists. These questioners and cynics and followers of new ideologies were the apikorsim, ("heretics") in the eyes of the religious majority.[11]

The common denominator of the various Jewish radical groups was not primarily their political philosophy since they represented several different varieties of socialism and Jewish nationalism, such as Zionism (Palestine homeland) and territorialism (cultural autonomy wherever possible). What brought them together was their fervent and almost universal desire to foster the Yiddish language. As Yiddishists they were virtually unanimous in the desire to develop Jewish schools emphasizing a Yiddish nationalist approach. The first of these schools were established in Montreal, Toronto and Winnipeg between 1910 and 1915. At the outset they were called the Jewish National Radical Schools.

The founders of these schools certainly held revolutionary views and the new approach to education represented an unprecedented departure from the established Hebrew religious schools. Inclusion of the word "radical" in the name of the schools however was really intended to emphasize their belief in the Yiddish language as basic and fundamental to the concept of the Jews as a national people. The realization that "radical" conveyed the impression of political extremism led the founders of these schools to change their name rather quickly to the Peretz

Schools, after I.L. Peretz, the classic Yiddish writer from Poland who gave vivid expression to the social ferment that affected Jewish life in those years.

The Peretz Schools did not have an easy time of it. Their supporters were denounced as heretics and apikorsim by the leaders of the Orthodox community and there were serious divisions within their own ranks. This was a period when Zionist ideology was also spreading and with it the interest in Hebrew as a modern language. In Montreal where the first radical or Peretz School was firmly established by the fall of 1913, Hebrew was included in the curriculum but it was not placed on an equal footing with Yiddish. The Labour Zionist element in the school quickly demanded equality for Hebrew and when they failed to achieve this they left and founded a second radical or progressive school. This school was opened in the fall of 1915 as the Jewish Peoples School or Folk Shule. There Hebrew would be taught equally with Yiddish from the first grade. The Peretz School did not introduce Hebrew until the third or fourth grade.

In Toronto the first Jewish National Radical School opened in 1911 and seems to have lasted continuously. Its experience in the early years was a little more serene than that of the school in Montreal. By 1917 the debate over Hebrew vs. Yiddish was repeated in Toronto and another school was established. Within two years, the two schools, both named after Peretz, got into financial difficulties and they were brought together under the auspices of the Arbeiter Ring, the Jewish Workmen's Circle, a fraternal organization.

In Winnipeg the Jewish Radical School was founded in 1914; some people didn't care for the designation "national" so it was left out of the name. A year later when it became the Peretz School, a more radical element broke away immediately and started a socialist Sunday school which lasted for about a year. By 1920 or 1921 this element had regrouped and organized an Arbeiter Ring Yiddish school.

Despite their internal divisions and external detractors the Peretz and Folk schools pioneered new approaches in Jewish education. The first kindergarten class in any Jewish school in North America was opened in the Folk Shule in Montreal in 1918. A year later a kindergarten was opened at the Winnipeg Peretz School by the Muter Farein ("mother's organization"). The Winnipeg effort was notable for the fact that as soon as the first kindergarten children reached the age of six the women moved immediately to establish a day school class which was the beginning of the first secular Jewish day school in North America, combining English language and general studies with the Jewish curriculum.

The achievement of the women in this pioneering kindergarten and day school grade class is noteworthy because the men did not expect it to succeed. These secular schools and the Reform religious schools were the first Jewish educational institutions in which women were able to take an equal part with the men. In Europe traditional Hebrew religious education had been the exclusive preserve of men and boys. Even in Canada, it was in the secular and Reform religious schools where girls were first able to take their place as students equally with boys. During the early years, however, the girl students in the secular schools outnumbered the boys by more than two to one. In the Winnipeg Peretz School in 1916 there were 127 girls and 58 boys, and in one Toronto school in 1918 there were 93 girls and 33 boys.

While many parents were prepared to send their children to the progressive schools, as they were known, some still wanted to have their sons prepared for Bar Mitzvah in the synagogue.[12] The near universal acceptance of Bar Mitzvah made it impossible for most progressive Jewish schools to maintain a complete break with religious instruction even if they wanted to. By 1917 all the major schools of secular persuasion were teaching Hebrew from the third grade. Eventually they started their own Bar Mitzvah classes for those parents who wanted it, and ultimately Bar Mitzvah studies became an established part of the curriculum for all boys in grade six as well as for those girls who wanted it.[13]

The intertwining of religion and history in Jewish tradition and experience makes it all but impossible for any Jewish school to be a-religious. Virtually every school in Canada founded by Jews who rejected religious practice had to concede, usually sooner than later, that no program of Jewish education could be carried on without imparting some knowledge of religion and its history. The most that these schools could do was to insist that religious practice was a private and personal matter. Nevertheless they were usually obliged to introduce religious instruction where parents desired it. The main difference therefore between the Talmud Torah, representing the religious stream, and the Peretz or Folk School, representing the secular, is that the former gives instruction in religious practice as something obligatory for all Jews, while the latter teaches religion and indicates that the degree of observance is a matter of family or personal choice.

Jewish schools, of course, do extend beyond the three cities whose educational experience has been particularly discussed. Day schools have also been established in Ottawa, Hamilton, Calgary, Edmonton and Vancouver and, in fact, in 1927 the Edmonton Talmud Torah became the first to establish a Hebrew religious day school in Canada. Only in Calgary and Vancouver, apart from the three main centres, is there more than one school to choose from. Some other cities, such as London and Windsor in the East, and Regina, Saskatoon and Victoria in the West still conduct regular afternoon schools, usually associated with the synagogue.

At one time every small Jewish town and every farm settlement also managed to conduct Hebrew classes. At least one farm settlement, Edenbridge, in northern Saskatchewan, conducted Yiddish secular studies as well as Hebrew classes because the forty to fifty families who farmed there included a free-thinkers group as well as a religious group. In one of the larger Jewish farm settlements, in the Lipton district, there were three schools because the population was scattered. They were also recognized as public schools and taught the general curriculum in addition to Judaic courses. The small town synagogues and schools have virtually disappeared in the 1970s, except for one or two in the West, at places like Thunder Bay and Prince Albert, and a few in the more populous East in the Niagara Peninsula and in northern Ontario.

The gradual disappearance of Jewish life in the small towns has been due not only to changing economic factors and the consequent inability to maintain schools and synagogues, but also due to the long-time pursuit of higher education by Jews no matter where they lived. By 1931 there were 1,626 Jewish university students in Canada representing one out of every 96 Jews out of the total Jewish population of just over 156,000. The total number of all university students in Canada that year was 32,783, representing 1 out of every 316 Canadians. By 1961 Jews in Canada had attained the highest average level of education of any ethnic group and their average length of school attendance was 10.1 years. There were 14,800 university educated Jews out of a total of 63,900 Jews in the labour force. With 23.2 percent of gainfully employed Jews having attended university, Jews in the labour force had the highest educational level of any of the major ethnic groups. The British were second with 11.5 percent.

There are several significant reasons for Canadian Jews being at the top of the educational ladder. When Jewish immigrants began coming to Canada in substantial numbers in the 1880s the overwhelming majority started at the bottom of the economic ladder. The average Jew was more mobile, however, than the average immigrant of any other background. The latter, whether he was a displaced peasant from Ireland or the Ukraine or even an unemployed craftsman or factory worker from England, was often so wedded to his social and economic position that it usually took him much longer to become upwardly mobile. Most Jewish parents were motivated by the idea of providing a good education for their children as soon as they arrived and were conditioned to make the necessary sacrifices from the outset.

Moreover during the first half of the twentieth century it was often not as easy for Jews as for other Canadians to enter university. At McGill University in Montreal, for example, Jewish students had to have higher average marks on high school graduation than non-Jewish students in order to be accepted. This meant that those Jewish students who did make the grade were from the outset closer to the top of the educational ladder than most non-Jews. In addition at some universities a quota system was enforced against Jews and members of some other minority groups seeking to enter medical schools. At the University of Manitoba Medical School, for instance, this quota system was not ended until Avukah, a Jewish student organization, mounted a public campaign in the early 1940s which brought the problem before the legislature. In summary it may be said that the unforeseen results of racial discrimination, added to the special striving of Jews for the best possible schooling, helped them to get to the top of the educational ladder.

Community Organization

Jewish life in Canada has followed a certain order of progression. First came the synagogue and burial society, followed by the cheder or religious school. Next came the benevolent society for charitable work and immigrant aid among those less fortunate. As the immigrants grew in numbers after 1890 they established *landsmanshaft* organizations, each one formed by a group of people who came from the same district or town. Apart from the founders these were not exclusive organizations but developed rather quickly into mutual benefit, sick benefit and free loan associations. The first Hebrew Ladies Association was formed in Victoria soon after the synagogue was built there in 1863, and the first women's groups in the East were started in Montreal, Toronto and Hamilton in 1877 and 1878. The first Canadian lodge of B'nai B'rith was established in Toronto in 1875.

By 1899 there were six local Zionist societies in Canada grouped together in a federation. And during the first fifteen years of the twentieth century, YMHAs were being opened as the Jewish counterpart of the YMCA; community homes for orphans and the aged were established in Montreal, Toronto and Winnipeg; and a health clinic and maternity hospital were opened in Montreal. During the First World War the Montreal and Toronto Jewish communities established the federations of Jewish charities. War relief activities were organized across the country, and the foundation was laid for the establishment of the Canadian Jewish Congress.

The oldest Jewish institution in Canada, and one which was the most important in the country before the First World War, is the Baron de Hirsch Institute and Hebrew Benevolent Society of Montreal. When the society was founded in 1863 as the Young Men's Hebrew Benevolent Society, the total Jewish population of Canada was less than a thousand and in Montreal was under four hundred. It took another seven or eight years until immigration reached one hundred a year. Nevertheless a group of thirty young men felt called upon to form an association "to assist their needy or unfortunate co-religionists." It was determined that the society should be "under the entire supervision and control of the young unmarried men of the city."

Six years later married co-religionists became eligible as members, and in 1870 the society became incorporated. It was not until 1882, however, with the arrival of over four hundred Russian Jews fleeing czarist persecution, that the YMHBs faced its first major challenge. Some aspects of the role of the society in the 1880s and 1890s have already been discussed. At the outset the organization was far from unanimous in rising to the challenge. While motivated by the Jewish tradition of philanthropy it reflected nevertheless the Canadian attitude of the day toward destitute families. As early as 1875 the YMHBs protested to the Ladies Emigration Aid Society in London, England, against the sending to Canada of immigrants and families "in a state of destitution . . . incapable of self-help."

In 1882 and 1883 the society became rather concerned about bearing the major responsibility of aid to newcomers. Some members felt that the Montreal community should not have to spend its own money to assist immigrants being sent to the West. The Mansion House Committee in London was asked for assistance, and early in 1883 the society passed a resolution threatening to send some immigrants back if no help came from London. The threat was not carried out, however, and help did come from London in the amount of twenty-five hundred dollars. With its treasury replenished the YMHBs began to extend its work, from direct relief to small business loans.

By 1890 the Young Men's Hebrew Benevolent Society of Montreal was thrust into the role of the first de facto national Jewish organization in Canada since it was processing virtually all Jewish immigrants destined to various parts of Canada and to some parts of the U.S. There was now a renewed upsurge of immigration, and the society found a new benefactor in the person of Baron Maurice de Hirsch, a wealthy European railway builder. Baron de Hirsch was well acquainted with the problems of his poverty stricken fellow-Jews in eastern Europe and was determined to help them find new homes and take up farming and other constructive occupations in other parts of the world. With the first twenty thousand dollar grant from Baron de Hirsch, the society decided to buy a building as a permanent shelter for newly arriving immigrants and to establish a school for immigrant children. The cost of the building was eight thousand dollars. It was the first Baron de Hirsch Institute.

No sooner was it launched on immigrant aid and education than the society found itself saddled with the responsibility of founding and managing a new Jewish farm settlement in the West. This was the Hirsch colony, started in 1892 with the financial support of the Jewish Colonization Association. (The JCA had been established that very year by Baron de Hirsch with the assistance of Jewish leaders in Paris and London.) The performance of the Montreal society in colonization work, however, proved to be the least satisfactory, and by 1902 the Jewish Colonization Association insisted on transferring responsibility for its Canadian colonies (another had been started at Lipton) to the Jewish Agricultural and Industrial Aid Society in New York. Five years later the responsibility was returned to Canada with the establishment of the Canadian Committee of the Jewish Colonization Association. The committee was headed by Mortimer B.

Davis (later Sir Mortimer) as chairman, Lyon Cohen was treasurer and S.W. Jacobs was secretary. Each of these men served in turn as president of the Baron de Hirsch Institute; they were the three most influential leaders of the Jewish community at that time. The new committee undertook the responsibility in 1907 "to disperse immigrants in places and towns in the Dominion and prevent congestion in Montreal." It also looked after the settlements under direct JCA auspices at Hirsch and Lipton and assisted Jewish farmers generally.

With this first transfer of a major area of responsibility to another organization the role of the Baron de Hirsch Institute was in no way diminished. At this very point (1902) the institute became involved in the legal defense of Jewish rights when it undertook to represent the Jewish community of Quebec in the school question which was taken to the courts and debated in the assembly. This crucial assignment was headed by Maxwell Goldstein, KC, who had been the honourary solicitor of the institute since the 1890s.

A few years later a campaign was undertaken to overcome the disability that would affect the Jews as a result of the Lord's Day Act which came before Parliament in Ottawa in 1906. Goldstein headed a Jewish deputation to Ottawa on this question, which included Toronto and Hamilton representatives, though the leadership came from Montreal.

The concern over the Lord's Day Act arose because its enactment would mean that Orthodox observant Jews, the vast majority of whom were at the bottom of the economic ladder, would be prevented from working on Sunday in addition to Saturday, the recognized Jewish Sabbath. The Jewish deputation succeeded in persuading the government to set up a select committee to consider whether the Lord's Day Act as drafted would do justice to all sections of the population. The deputation then convinced the committee to propose an amendment granting exemption to any group that conscientiously observed Saturday as the Sabbath, so long as any Sunday work done would not be disturbing to Christian neighbours. There was great opposition to the proposed exemption for the Jews particularly from the Lord's Day Alliance. When the matter came before the House of Commons, thirty-nine members took part in the debate and many of them admitted that this was the first time the Jewish side of the question had been explained to them. The amendment was finally defeated seventy-nine to fifty-seven, but it represented a considerable moral victory for the Jewish deputation. Twenty members including Prime Minister Laurier and three other Cabinet ministers spoke in favour of the amendment, as compared with two Cabinet ministers and the leader of the Opposition, Robert Borden, who were among nineteen vocal opponents. All French Canadian and Quebec members who took part in the debate supported the amendment.

The Lord's Day Act as finally adopted did permit the provinces to introduce modifying regulations within their own jurisdiction. It is therefore not surprising to find that Catholic Quebec, where attendance at Mass was considered sufficient Sunday observance, enacted a provincial law which granted the exemption requested by the Jews. (This is why author Ted Allen, as a boy of six, was able to join his grandfather on Sunday peddling excursions and later to write a story about it which has grown into the outstanding full-length Canadian movie, *Lies My Father Told Me.*)

After the experience with the Lord's Day Act, the Baron de Hirsch Institute established a legislative committee (February 1909) headed by Maxwell Goldstein to play a similar role in future regarding legislation that might affect Jewish interests. It was recognized that there was a need to make the committee representative of all Jewish organizations and it was even visualized as a step toward a board of deputies for Jews throughout Canada.

One special problem which the legislative committee dealt with was a defamation case which began after a Quebec City notary and journalist, J.E. Plamondon, made a speech accusing the Jews of "ritual murder" and sundry other "crimes," deriving his information from anti-Jewish mythology. The speech was published in pamphlet form, aggravating the situation and creating a hostile atmosphere in the city. A number of Jews were molested, windows were broken in several private homes and in the synagogue during a service. Several young men were arrested, charged and found guilty of damaging the synagogue and the Jewish homes. The convictions were considered insufficient, however, and it was decided to take the matter to court to prove the falsehood of Plamondon's charges.

Benzion Ortenberg and Louis Lazarovitch, the latter president of the synagogue, launched a civil libel action against Plamondon and his publisher, and S.W. Jacobs, KC, took the case at the behest of the legislative committee. The action was dismissed twice in the lower courts, but on appeal to the Quebec Court of Appeals the earlier judgments were overturned and the plaintiffs' charge sustained. The decision was based on the fact that since there were only seventy-five Jewish families in Quebec City each one of them might have considered themselves personally libelled by Plamondon. This meant, however, that the appeal court decision would not stand as a group libel precedent.

In 1900 the Baron de Hirsch Institute obtained a new charter granting it powers to provide relief to the "sick and indigent," to establish "a home or refuge for the distressed, aged and orphans," to provide a burial ground for the poor, conduct schools, found a cadet corps, assist immigrants and settlers all over the country and to maintain charitable, philanthropic and patriotic works. Without underestimating the varied and unusual work which was done by this first Jewish social welfare body in Canada it soon became clear that the institute could not, in fact, meet all needs and satisfy the many diverse elements that were to be found in the Jewish community after 1900. The next fifteen years have been called the golden age of the Baron de Hirsch Institute but the institute was already in a decline.

The relief department developed into the family and child welfare agency for which the institute is noted to this day; the burial ground established by the agency still serves the community, as does the legal aid department. The homes for orphans and the aged, however, as well as the health clinic and maternity hospital were all founded as independent institutions at the instigation of newcomers. The primary responsibility for settlement of immigrants across the country was removed from the institute almost as soon as it received its new charter powers, though it was directly represented in the establishment of the Canadian branch of the Jewish Colonization Association. Even when a group of Jewish leaders closely involved with the Baron de Hirsch Institute took the lead in establishing the Mount Sinai Sanatorium (for the treatment of tuberculosis), it was an independent agency from the outset.

Many of the newcomers who were motivated to establish their own self-help organizations looked upon the leaders of the Baron de Hirsch Institute as the "uptown Jews." While they were not necessarily averse to working with the institute, they wished to do so as equals and not as supplicants. This was particularly apparent with regard to the school question. A separate Jewish school system, similar to that of the Protestants and Catholics in Quebec, was actually favoured by many newcomers. Simon Belkin[14] writes that the Baron de Hirsch School started in the 1890s might have become the foundation for a Jewish separate school system but the leaders of the school were opposed to the idea. Harris Vineberg, a president of the institute during its ascendance, explained that many immigrant children were ashamed to enter the general schools on their arrival because they knew no English. The Baron de Hirsch school thus became a kind of preparatory school; it ceased to operate as such by 1914.

In 1902 the Baron de Hirsch Institute opened its Bleury Street building which became a community landmark in Montreal for the next half century. In its early years it also served as a social and cultural centre. Considering the many new Jewish organizations, agencies and institutions established during this period, not only in Montreal but throughout Canada, it may be suggested that the religious concept of the minyan, the prayer

quorum for a congregation, was carried over into secular activities. Not unexpectedly some members of the establishment group, the uptown Jews, could neither understand nor appreciate this approach.

Maxwell Goldstein, for example, who had rendered valuable service as chairman of the legislative committee, told the London *Jewish Chronicle,* during a 1909 visit to Britain, "the cause of many of our troubles is the vast influx of foreign Jews into the Dominion." Being president of the Reform Temple at the time, Goldstein was concerned that many newcomers "not only formed congregations of their own," which were of course Orthodox, but that they even appointed "a foreign Chief Rabbi for themselves. . . ." He suggested, "the only thing to do is to take them by the hand and lead them by persuasive methods to recognize their duties to the community."

A few weeks later, Lyon Cohen, then president of the Baron de Hirsch Institute, was interviewed in London by the same publication and spoke in a manner far different from Goldstein's biased and condescending approach. Where Goldstein had said the newcomers "form ghettos among themselves and create a great deal of prejudice," Cohen spoke of the concern "to avoid the creation of ghettos [and the] problems which congested Jewish districts involve," referring to health problems among the poor. Goldstein appeared to welcome the recent immigration restrictions which caused a lessening in immigration as a welcome restraint that might allow time "to assimilate and consolidate all sections of the community." Cohen warned against "wholesale emigration" to Canada but added that the country could absorb large numbers provided they come gradually "to enable us to deal with them systematically [and] do justice to individual requirements."[15]

On returning home Lyon Cohen was queried by the *Canadian Jewish Times* as to whether the London paper had asked him some of the other questions on which Goldstein had commented. Cohen responded that he had refused to answer a question about relations between Orthodox and Reform in Montreal because it was a domestic issue that he felt should not have been discussed abroad. Being himself a leader and future president of the still Orthodox Shaar Hashomayim Synagogue, Cohen added, "Orthodoxy's failure to appreciate Reform is certainly good."

On retiring as president of the Baron de Hirsch Institute in 1912, Lyon Cohen put forward the need to establish a federation or union to coordinate all the charitable institutions that had developed in Montreal during the past decade. Two years later he was named chairman of the committee which laid the groundwork for the establishment of the Federation of Jewish Philanthropies of Montreal. When the federation came into being on 1 January 1917, it had twelve founding agencies, including the Baron de Hirsch Institute, Mount Sinai Sanatorium, Herzl Dispensary and Hospital, the Montreal Hebrew Orphans Home and the Montreal Hebrew Sheltering Home. The others were all agencies and organizations of special concern to women, such as the Ladies Jewish Endeavor Sewing School, the Young Women's Hebrew Association and the Beth Israel Day Nursery and Infants Home. The object of the federation was not only to seek coordination and to avoid duplication of services but to unite for the purposes of fund raising. In this regard the Montreal Jewish federation was the first united fund-raising organization for charitable purposes for all of Canada and established a precedent not only for other Jewish communities but for the community at large.

The Montreal federation had been officially incorporated by an act of the Quebec legislature in March 1916, and provisional officers were elected a month later. The first campaign, however, was not started until early in January 1917. In Toronto where a temporary organizing committee was not called together until the end of October 1916, they moved much more quickly and began their fund-raising campaign in mid-February 1917. The first campaign of the Jewish federation in Montreal brought in some one hundred and twenty-five thousand dollars, representing about 65 percent more than the total income of the founding constituent groups in the previous year. In Toronto the first campaign brought in close to thirty thousand dollars. Montreal's Jewish population was around forty-four thousand at the time while Toronto stood at about thirty-three thousand, but the upper echelon of Montreal Jewry was certainly more prosperous.

Another factor which surely motivated the drive towards united fund-raising efforts was the changed relationship between the organized Jewish community in Canada and their counterparts in Europe. Before the First World War Canadian Jewish organizations had continued to look to the Anglo-Jewish Association in Britain and the Jewish Colonization Association, in London and Paris, as their parent bodies. The JCA in particular was still sending financial aid for farm settlement. The war put an end to this and marked the beginning of fund raising efforts by Jews in Canada for overseas aid. Before discussing this phase of organized Jewish activity in Canada it is necessary to turn back once more to the nineteenth century to examine the beginnings of the Zionist movement and to consider the early involvement in it of Canadian Jews.

To discuss the development of Canadian Jewish interest in and support for Zionism in the aftermath of the United Nations resolution of November 1975, which presumed to label Zionism as racism, it is necessary to go back into history to see how both terms arose. The rise of modern racism, which has so marred the history of the twentieth century, is traced back to two nineteenth century ideologues, Count Joseph Arthur de Gobineau, a Frenchman, and Houston Stewart Chamberlain, an Anglo-German. (The latter was born in England, educated in France and Germany, and became a German citizen after he married Richard Wagner's daughter.) De Gobineau was the first to attribute a scale of cultural values to the races of mankind with the Nordic group at the top. Chamberlain claimed that the Nordic and Teutonic people, especially the Germans, were the master race and proclaimed a crusade against the Jews. His father-in-law, Wagner, supported him by writing a pamphlet against Judaism in music!

The concept of political Zionism as a movement to re-establish a Jewish state homeland in Palestine also had its origins in the mid-nineteenth century. It was conceived by Jewish thinkers who saw the rise of modern anti-Semitism, spurred by the theory of racism in the midst of the era of "enlightenment" and Jewish emancipation in western Europe. Moses Hess, a German Jew who was a proponent of humanitarianism and a Hegelian philosopher, is considered the theoretical father of modern Zionism. The Italian liberation movement of Garibaldi and Mazzini fired Hess with the idea of a similar Jewish liberation movement which he expounded in one of his books *Rome and Jerusalem* (1862).

Moses Hess called for "an end to all caste spirit and all class rule" and he proclaimed that "humanity is a living organism, of which races and peoples are the members." He considered that the Jews had a "historic and cultural vocation to unite man and his world and to create human brotherhood" and he linked this with the belief that "this people has preserved its nationality *within* its religion and has connected both inseparably with the inalienable land of its fathers."

The Zionist movement which developed after Hess died adopted this messianic interpretation and, whether or not one finds it personally acceptable, it must surely be seen as the very antithesis of the theory of racism. Zionism today may have lost some of its messianic zeal, but, except through the crassest opportunism, it can hardly be equated with the very thesis it was set to oppose.

The first attempt to establish a Zionist group in Canada occurred in Montreal in 1892. Some fifty people enrolled but only one of the first officers, Lazarus Cohen, had any association with the established Jewish leadership of that day. He was very concerned with the resettlement of Jews from eastern Europe and early in 1893 undertook a mission to Palestine together with a represen-tative of the Zionist society of New York. Lazarus Cohen came back inspired by the great possibilities of Jewish settlement in Palestine. He was not blinded to the tremendous obstacles that stood in the way and the sacrifices that would be required. His forthright appraisal of the situation led many weak-hearted members to abandon the Zionist group. Some tentative efforts were continued during the next few years with little success. In January 1898, six months after Theodor Herzl convened the first World Zionist Congress in Basle, Switzerland, a Zionist mass meeting took place in a Montreal synagogue and within a month a provisional committee had been established with representatives from every synagogue except the Reform Temple. Lazarus Cohen was there, of course, representing the Shaar Hashomayim.[16]

It is well known that it was the presence of Theodor Herzl in Paris at the trial of Captain Alfred Dreyfus, (the Jewish army officer falsely accused and convicted of treason and condemned to life imprisonment on Devil's Island) that changed the assimilated Austrian Jew into the founder of the World Zionist Organization. The Dreyfus case had a world-wide influence which could hardly escape the Jews or the general community of Montreal. (Dreyfus was retried and convicted a second time in 1899, with extenuating circumstances acknowledged. He was not declared innocent by the French court until 1906.) One of the leading French-language journalists in Montreal during this period was Jules Helbronner, an Alsatian Jew, who became editor of Montreal's leading French daily, *La Presse,* in the 1890s and wrote numerous editorials in defense of Dreyfus.

The Zionist Society of Montreal was established in March 1898, with a constitution based on the program of the first World Zionist Congress, (1) to promote the acquisition of a publicly secured, legally assured home for the Jewish people in Palestine; (2) to promote the settlement in Palestine of Jews engaged in agriculture, handicrafts, industries and professions; (3) to centralize the Jewish people by means of general and local institutions, agreeable to the laws of the land where they reside;

(4) to strengthen Jewish national consciousness and sentiment;
(5) to obtain the sanction of governments to carry out the objects of Zionism. The first of these objectives was brought to a climactic stage when Britain issued the Balfour Declaration in 1917.

It is noteworthy that the first president of the Zionist society in Montreal was Dr. David A. Hart, a great-grandson of Aaron Hart. Lazarus Cohen was first vice-president. The Federation of Zionist Societies was established in November 1899, with Clarence I. de Sola (a son of Rabbi Abraham de Sola) as president. The first Canadian Zionist convention took place in Montreal in December 1900; there were now ten local societies from Saint John, New Brunswick, in the East, to Winnipeg in the West. The following year at the second convention the first women delegates were in attendance.

Zionism has always been regarded as a unique Jewish form of modern nationalism. Almost from the outset it developed divergent trends due to the influence of other ideologies. While Zionism drew its inspiration for the return to the ancient homeland in Palestine from Biblical and religious teachings, some Jewish religious leaders opposed Zionism at the outset. The ultra-Orthodox opposed it because they could not exchange their belief in the coming of a divinely chosen Messiah for the idea of a man-made messianic age. Apparently none of Montreal's Orthodox synagogues was so ultra as to remain aloof when the first Zionist society was founded in Canada. The Reform movement opposed Zionism before the First World War because it could not reconcile Judaism as a religion with Jewish nationalism. There were notable exceptions to this view from the outset among leading reform rabbis such as Dr. Stephen S. Wise, who was a founder of the Zionist Organization of America.

In 1905 as the federation, renamed the Canadian Zionist Federation, was holding its fourth convention, the establishment of new societies at Brandon and at the Wapella farm settlement was reported. At the same time a group of recent immigrants was taking steps to organize the first Poale Zion ("workers of Zion") group in Montreal. This was the beginning of the Labour Zionist Organization in Canada, representing the Socialist Zionist Party. The Zionist movement was by this time developing its own parties of the right, left and centre, and the Zionist Federation of Canada soon came to occupy the centre. By 1915 the Mizrachi ("religious") Zionist organization was established in Canada; it was generally considered as being to the right. In the next decade, however, there developed Hapoel Hamizrachi, a religious Labour Zionist organization, and by 1930 Canada had a branch of the Revisionist Zionist organization which was clearly to the right. It will thus be seen that in the development of Zionism as a form of Jewish nationalism, just as in the development of religious and educational trends in Judaism, the Jewish people were never monolithic.

It is now time to consider the move for unity for the purpose of seeking certain central objectives in the organized Jewish community. The achievement of a significant measure of unity for local welfare needs through the Montreal and Toronto Jewish federations has already been discussed. At the same time the First World War brought forward the challenge of organizing relief for Jewish war sufferers. It also gave rise to the larger problem of seeking to develop a unified approach to secure and defend the rights of Jewish people everywhere after the war.

Discussion of the need for a war relief campaign began in Montreal and Toronto in November 1914, but active fund-raising efforts did not begin in those cities until the spring of 1915. The first collections in Canada for Jewish war relief took place at the Lipton farm settlement in Saskatchewan and in Winnipeg during October 1914. Activities were delayed in the East and a hiatus also developed in Winnipeg because of the view that the war might end in short order. This was soon dispelled and a united campaign effort was launched in Montreal early in 1915 which raised about twenty-four thousand dollars. Dissension arose over the distribution of funds when the "uptown" group, which constituted a majority of the campaign committee, decided that local charitable organizations should get first call on the funds because their position had been weakened by the commercial depression which affected Canadian business following the outbreak of hostilities.

The leadership of the "downtown" Jews had a more immediate feeling for the needs of its brothers and sisters overseas from whom they had been removed but a few short years. A conference was convened in late February 1915, by the Labour Zionist and fraternal labour groups, all of which had been organized during the previous decade. At this conference it was decided to establish the Folks Farband, the Canadian Jewish Alliance, and for the first time there was a call for a Canadian Jewish congress. Immediate steps were also taken to raise relief funds on a regular basis, all of which would go to Jews in need of aid in Europe and in Palestine, which had become a theatre of war. The uptown Jews, not to be outdone, organized the Canadian Jewish Committee, also for the purpose of raising funds exclusively for overseas relief. Several other war relief groups were started in Montreal including the Central Relief Committee, representing a number of synagogues, the Ukrainian Verband or Alliance of Ukrainian Jews, as well as a Romanian and Russian-Polish group. Each one operated independently during most of the war years but there was a gradual move towards a united effort which eventually materialized.

In Toronto the same situation did not develop because the Labour Zionists and associated groups, led by Morris Goldstick, were able to bring together all organizations and synagogues concerned with war relief under the umbrella of the Toronto Conference for Jewish War Sufferers.

The initiative in Winnipeg was taken in 1915 by a group called the Young Maccabees. It succeeded in convening a meeting of thirty-five different organizations for the purpose of organizing a war relief alliance. Within a year this grew into the Western Jewish Fund for the Relief of War Sufferers. Under the chairmanship of Marcus Hyman it won the affiliation of virtually every Jewish community and organization throughout the West.

By 1919 the various Montreal groups together with the Toronto conference and the Western Canada Fund came together to establish the Associated Jewish War Relief Societies of Canada.

War relief activities burgeoned throughout Canada and young Jewish men were enlisted in the armed forces. In the last year of the war the authorities granted permission for the recruiting of volunteers to serve in a Jewish brigade with General Allenby in Palestine. The most important development for Jewish life in Canada was the movement to convene the first Canadian Jewish Congress. This came about as part of a movement by Jewish communities and organizations in many countries to establish a world Jewish congress to defend the rights of Jews wherever they lived as well as to mobilize greater support for a Jewish homeland in Palestine.

In Canada the first serious efforts for a congress were initiated by men like Reuben Brainin, a Yiddish-Hebrew author and journalist, and Dr. Yehudah Kaufman, an educator, both of whom were active supporters of Labour Zionism. They began to promote the idea of a Canadian Jewish congress through the Folks Farband ("Canadian Jewish Alliance") of which they became the leaders in Montreal in 1915. Once again there was a serious difference with the leaders of the uptown Jews, this time represented by Clarence de Sola, president of the Zionist Federation. The Folks Farband wanted a congress, elected by popular franchise, to work for national rights for Jews everywhere. The de Sola element of the Zionist Federation wanted a conference of Jewish organizational representatives to seek the emancipation of their unfortunate brethren in Europe.

The Folks Farband succeeded in organizing a branch in Toronto, headed by Morris Goldstick, who was already leading the war relief work, and it also won considerable support in Winnipeg where the Committee for the Removal of the Disabilities of the Jews was established in 1915. Again it was in the West that the first significant move towards unity came. The Winnipeg group established a strong congress committee and organized a widely representative western conference which took place in Winnipeg in August 1916. A total of 205 delegates representing eighteen western centres were in attendance. M.J. Finkelstein, the leading Winnipeg representative of the Zionist Federation, took a prominent part in the conference along with men like J.A. Cherniack, a socialist territorialist turned Labour Zionist, and Ben Sheps, president of Winnipeg's Hebrew Immigration Aid Society.

The Winnipeg conference called for a Canadian Jewish congress to take place as soon as possible and favoured the popular representation advocated by the Montreal Folks Farband. It was not until the end of 1918, however, that the move to unity was successful in Montreal and Toronto. At that time a plan was agreed upon to convene the congress in Montreal. A Canada-wide election of delegates took place on March 2 and 3, 1919, in which 24,866 votes were cast to elect 209 delegates, from Glace Bay, Nova Scotia to Vegreville, Alberta, to the founding convention of the Canadian Jewish Congress which was to open on March 16. The large number of votes cast is significant because it meant that almost every adult Jew in Canada had voted, demonstrating the universal interest in the idea of a Jewish congress.

The convention discussions went on for three and a half days and featured the question of a Jewish homeland in Palestine and equal rights for Jews everywhere, including Canada. There were also major discussions on immigration, on Jewish education and there was even an address on the five-day work week. The most practical results of the congress were the planning of continued war relief and intensified immigrant aid.

There was agreement on the establishment of a permanent congress and Lyon Cohen, probably the most understanding of the uptown Jews was elected president. H.M. Caiserman, a stalwart of the Labour Zionist organization, became general secretary. Following the convention the congress and its associated groups across the country soon became involved in sending briefs, telegrams and letters to Ottawa concerning the problems of the Jews in Europe and particularly the persecution being suffered by Polish and Ukrainian Jews as a result of the revolutionary upheavals in that part of the world as the war ended.

Probably the most important result of the first congress was the establishment of a national Jewish immigrant aid program across the country. This was urgently required to help Jews come to Canada in the face of growing immigration restrictions. In the early 1920s, however, the congress fell into a hiatus and it was not revived to become a truly permanent and effective national organization until Hitler's Fascism loomed large on the horizon in 1933.

The delegates to the Canadian Jewish Congress of 1919 represented every shade of opinion not only in Jewish life but in Canadian life as a whole, and they ranged from right wing Conservatives to left wing Social Democrats. Nevertheless they were able to achieve virtual unanimity on vital matters of common concern to them as Jews. Most significant among the resolutions adopted was the one presented to the convention by the Palestine Committee. The resolution called for sending Canadian delegates to the European Peace Conference to cooperate with all other Jewish organizations in seeking the recognition of the Peace Conference for the historic claims of the Jewish people in Palestine. It asked for the establishment of a Palestine administration under British trusteeship to develop the country in accordance with the British government's declaration of 2 November 1917 (the Balfour Declaration),

through a Jewish Commonwealth, it being clearly understood that nothing shall be done which shall prejudice the civil, national and religious rights of the existing non-Jewish communities in Palestine, or the rights and political status enjoyed by Jews in any other country.

Louis Fitch of Montreal presented the resolution and its adoption was moved by M.J. Finkelstein of Winnipeg who asked that it be carried unanimously. S. Almazoff, another Winnipeg delegate, described as an extreme anti-national socialist rose to speak amidst vociferous opposition from the floor. When the chairman persuaded the convention to allow him to speak, Almazoff said in part,

> I, too, see Palestine as a Jewish home, but I see it under the only conditions it can become a Jewish homeland, when the whole structure of society has been changed. I am not in agreement with the resolution; nevertheless I shall not vote against it. I do not believe that the imperialistic ambitions of Great Britain or of France can help the Jewish people. Nevertheless your faith is beautiful, and I do not know whether you ought to envy me, or I ought to envy you.

Almazoff's speech was greeted with almost reverential silence. He was supported by one Montreal delegate, Joseph Shubert, who shared his affiliation and echoed his views, concluding with praise for the toleration shown by the congress. The resolution was then adopted without a dissenting vote.

Before the convention ended it also passed unanimously a resolution calling for a five-day work week. This question had been introduced by Rabbi J. Gordon of Toronto, described as a representative of the conservative Jewish element. The majority support of the congress for improved labour conditions was clear. The delegates to the convention included many shop workers and union members as well as those who were manufacturers, factory owners or lawyers who served business interests. Two months after the convention some of the Winnipeg delegates found themselves on opposite sides in the General Strike that broke out in mid-May. All Jewish factory workers were, of course, among the strikers. Max Steinkopf, a corporation lawyer who had been a delegate to the congress convention, became a member of the anti-strike Committee of 1000. Abraham Heaps, an English Jew who was then a member of Winnipeg City Coun-

cil, was arrested along with the other English strike leaders (R.B. Russell, John Queen, etc), and S. Almazoff, the Social Democratic delegate to the congress convention, was one of the strikers arrested and held for deportation for no other reason than that they all had foreign-sounding names. Almazoff persuaded the authorities not to deport him but later moved to New York.

There are indications that Jews were actively involved in Canadian trade unions as early as the 1890s and that the first union local of Jewish tailors was organized in Montreal under the auspices of the Knights of Labour. The tailors very soon joined the United Garment Workers Union and it is reported that in 1895 the Canadian Trades and Labour Congress passed a resolution on the request of United Garment Workers Union Local No. 81 to ask the Canadian government to investigate the sweat shop system. Some Jewish manufacturers were operating sweat shops but this did not stop Jewish workers from joining the campaign against the sweat system.

This essay began by following up Sir John A. Macdonald's 1882 prediction that the Jews being sent to the West to farm would go in for peddling and politics. From that point Jewish life in Canada has been delineated through its occupational, religious, educational, ideological and community organizational developments. It has come full circle to those important dates in 1919 which marked the first gathering of the Canadian Jewish community for common purposes yet at the same time demonstrated how individual Jews play their roles as Canadians in whatever walks of life they find themselves. It remains now but to sum up with a commentary on where the Jews stand today in Canadian life.

The Jewish Community Today

According to the 1971 census there were two hundred and seventy-six thousand Jews living in Canada.[17] In this decade, the tenth since Jewish immigration exceeded one hundred per year, the total number may approach three hundred thousand. About one-third of the Jewish population of Canada are post-World War II immigrants or their children — survivors or descendants of survivors of the Nazi holocaust in which six million Jews perished. If Canada and many other countries of the world had not taken such a callous attitude toward the Jews who were trying to leave Germany and other European countries after Hitler came to power in the 1930s there is no doubt that hundreds of thousands and possibly millions may have been saved.

From 1921 to 1930 Canada admitted an average of five thousand Jewish immigrants per year. From 1931 to 1940 as the threatening clouds loomed and the terrible storm burst upon Europe in its unimaginable fury, the number of Jews admitted to Canada dropped to an average of five hundred per year. Had the policy of admitting refugee immigrants on compassionate grounds been introduced before the Second World War, as it should have been, Canada might have saved at least another fifty thousand people simply by allowing Jews to come in at the same rate during the thirties as during the twenties. Yet, even during the 1920s it was extremely difficult for Jews to come to Canada because of the restrictive immigration regulations. It took a great deal of intensive effort and special pleading on the part of the organized Jewish community to open Canada's doors to those who did come during that period.

When discussions were taking place in the late 1930s about trying to save some of the Jews of Germany, Prime Minister Mackenzie King and his immigration officials repeatedly stated that they were not prepared to ease the very strict immigration regulations which had been introduced when Canada was hit by the depression. King even said at one point that no organization in Canada was prepared to undertake responsibility for the refugees who wanted to come. This was simply not true.

In 1938 the Canadian Jewish Congress, with the active assistance of the three Jewish members of Parliament (S.W. Jacobs, A.A. Heaps and Sam Factor), launched a special effort to persuade the Canadian government to admit an increased but selective number of refugee Jews from Germany. The response they received was lukewarm, to put it mildly. In June of that year Prime Minister King, acting as Secretary of State for External Affairs, addressed a private memo to H.H. Wrong, Canada's permanent delegate to the League of Nations, on the proposed conference on refugees to be held at Evian, France, that summer. The main problem was how to help Jewish refugees. In his memo to Wrong the Prime Minister said, among other things, "thus far we have not received any evidence of a willingness, on the part of private organizations in Canada to become financially responsible for any immigrants though the situation may change. . . ." He also suggested that since "the majority of the Jewish immigrants now resident in Canada are natives of Poland, Russia and Romania rather than of Austria or Germany, . . . the interest of this Jewish population is therefore centered on Eastern rather than on Central Europe." This memorandum was sent out just three weeks after the Prime Minister had met with a delegation comprising the three Jewish MPs together with two other MPs, J.S. Woodsworth and Col. T.A. Vien, "in reference to the question of political and religious refugees from Austria and Germany," as A.A. Heaps reported to Alderman M.A. Gray in Winnipeg on 25 May 1938.

Moreover just two years earlier on 18 February 1936, the Jewish Immigrant Aid Society had written a letter to Thomas A. Crerar, Minister of Immigration, confirming an earlier discussion with him about the problem of the Jews in Germany and asking that Canada do something about it by admitting "a small number of specially and carefully selected men [who] would not materially accentuate the present employment situation." Expressing the hope for early action so that "at least some suffering might be mitigated" the organization gave a commitment to undertake not only to distribute the immigrants throughout the country but "to properly take care of them, and to prevent any of them from becoming a charge on the public." This very clear commitment was signed for the society by Lyon Cohen, by S.W. Jacobs, MP, who had succeeded Cohen as president of the Canadian Jewish Congress, by Samuel Bronfman, who had already emerged as a national leader, by A.J. Freiman of Ottawa, who had been national president of the Zionist Organization of Canada (formerly the Canadian Zionist Federation) since 1919, by Heaps and Factor, the two other Jewish MPs, and by Benjamin Robinson, president of the Jewish Immigrant Aid Society. And what was the result? In the fiscal year 1935-36 the number of Jewish immigrants to Canada was 880; in the next two years it dropped to 619 and 584.

In 1938 there was absolutely no doubt in the minds of the national refugee committee of the Canadian Jewish Congress as to the countries from which they wanted to bring Jewish immigrants. They were also clearly aware, and certainly conveyed their understanding to King and to Crerar, who was still the minister responsible, that the Jewish community would undertake full financial responsibility for any Jewish immigrants. The result of these efforts, one year before the war broke out, caused A.A. Heaps to charge that the existing immigration regulations were "inhuman and anti-Christian." In a letter to the Prime Minister he also told him "the sentiment is gaining ground that anti-Semitic influences are responsible for the government's refusal to allow refugees to come to Canada."

From 1882 onward there was always some representative body of the Jewish community prepared to guarantee that Jewish immigrants would not become a public charge, as required by law for all immigrants. Moreover after the founding convention of the Canadian Jewish Congress in 1919, the one proposal that was carried out before all others was the establishment of a national Jewish Immigrant Aid Society with active branches in centres from coast to coast.

If the Canadian government had followed a policy of true compassion during the decade now known as the "dirty thirties," instead of displaying anti-Semitic prejudice, thinly veiled by legalistic excuses and lame criticism of Jewish organizations in Canada, then this country might have saved fifty thousand, one hundred thousand and possibly even two hundred thousand of the people who lost their lives in Nazi gas chambers. The 1930s era was clearly more than "dirty"; it was a decade of despair for people who were trying to escape the coming holocaust in Europe and for those who knew it was coming and were frustrated in their efforts to save them.

This decade of despair, which kept a tight lid on the Jewish population, also created a social and economic pressure cooker in which anti-Semitic prejudice and racial discrimination in higher education and employment were some of the conditions with which Canadian Jews had to contend. These conditions in the 1930s contributed to placing the Jews in the 1960s as a group at or near the top of the ladder of statistical averages in education and economic status, though individually most are below the average. At the same time the Jewish group has moved to the bottom of the numerical ladder of the ten largest ethnocultural groups in the country.

In December 1975, an economic study of the one hundred

and ten thousand Jews living in Montreal, Canada's major Jewish population centre, showed that at least eighteen thousand are living below the poverty line of $5,000 per year for a family of four, as defined by the Canadian Senate. Montreal's Jewish poor comprise three groups, the aged who didn't make it when others were moving to the top, the working poor at the bottom of the educational and vocational ladder who include many postwar immigrants, and a large section of Montreal's fifteen thousand observant Orthodox Jews. Many in the latter category belong to the Chasidic Jewish community of whom the great majority are postwar immigrants.

In the Canada of the 1970s Jews perceive themselves in different ways depending to a considerable extent on their personal status in society. More and more, their view of themselves also depends on their appreciation of history, and in this regard the history of the past thirty to forty years is having a great effect. The survivor of the holocaust of World War II almost invariably feels that his experience was so inexpressibly terrible and unique that it is incomparable with any other devasting visitation, such as the atom bomb on Hiroshima, the Viet Nam War or the tribal destruction in Biafra or Bangladesh. Some Jews who witnessed the immediate aftermath of the holocaust as members of the Canadian forces in Europe, or who lived through the war in Canada, share these feelings, partly from a sense of unease or even guilt at not having personally experienced the Ghetto and the death camps. Many of those born after World War II including some of the children of holocaust survivors, along with more rational members of the war generation find this view hard to understand. They believe that, for people who did not live through it, the horrors of the holocaust must be shown in perspective with more recent cataclysmic visitations.

This view of the past within memory, coupled with the apparent continued threats to the survival of the State of Israel, contributes to a feeling of insecurity among many Canadian Jews. While this feeling must be understood, nevertheless in the view of this writer it leads to a banal ritual, often repeated at Jewish community gatherings, which rejects the notion "it can't happen here" and replaces it with the cry "never again!" This is applied to the situation of Israel today, to the problem of the Jews in the Soviet Union, and sometimes — it is surely incredible — to the situation right here in Canada!

This may well have been a underlying factor contributing to the excessive reaction of some sections of the Jewish community to the idea of delegates of the Palestine Liberation Organization coming to Canada to attend a UN conference. The UN anti-Zionist resolution of November 1975, has added fuel to these blazing emotions.

At the same time the position which the individual Jew may achieve in Canadian society today should provide at least part of the answer to these feelings. Consider the fact that it was the responsibility of Barney Danson, a Jew, in his role as Minister of Urban Affairs, to defend the government's position regarding the Habitat Conference of 1976 and the attendance of a PLO delegation. At the same time, Senator Sidney Buckwold, another Jew, was serving as chairman of the Canadian National Committee for Habitat and in that role acting as the leading proponent for Canadian participation in the conference.

The attitudes of the Jews vary from unique emotional feelings, sometimes reaching to paranoia, to the universalist concept which sustains some Jews whose formal affiliation with the Jewish community may be tenuous at best. The founder of modern Orthodoxy, Samson Raphael Hirsch, proclaimed the universal brotherhood of mankind as Israel's most cherished ideal (1836). And Moritz Lazarus, a German-Jewish philosopher of the enlightenment declared, "Israel had to be particularistic in order to formulate and hold up in the universal ideal" (1901).

In Canada today Jewish people live under conditions of freedom which have not been exceeded anywhere in the world including the State of Israel. There are those who argue that only in Israel can a Jew live in full freedom as a Jew. This may be so for those who want a very particular kind of Jewish life. The great majority of Canadian Jews, however, whether they are Orthodox, Conservative or Reform, whether or not they belong to a Zionist organization or hold any other formal Jewish affiliation, are certain that they intend to remain in Canada. Even for those Jews whose emotional reactions to recent events has led them to march and demonstrate and vent their feelings aloud, their ability to do so is but further evidence of the high degree of freedom enjoyed in Canada.

It is also significant that many who consider themselves secular Jews — or universalists if you will — have come to share with acknowledged religious Jews the feeling of commitment to Israel as a spiritual or cultural homeland even if they have no intention of settling there. Moreover many with the most tenous commitment or affiliation have also been shaken by recent world events and have begun to share the view that the survival of Israel, with its inevitable human blemishes and shortcomings, has a profound importance for every self-acknowledged Jew.

Jewish life in Canada in the best sense has been a creative force over the years and the results are evident not only in the synagogues and schools but in the YMHAs and community centres, libraries and performing groups. The YM-YWHA and the Jewish Public Library in Montreal have been exemplary institutions in fostering the cultural arts and literary activities to this very day. Jewish education has moved to the academic level in recent years with Jewish studies programs in many universities. Here again Winnipeg pioneered in the 1950s with the establishment of the Judaic Studies Department at the University of Manitoba, now the Department of Near East and Judaic Studies. In spite of the receding of Yiddish as a spoken tongue, Montreal has had a flourishing amateur Yiddish theatre company for some twenty-five years, originally fostered through the Jewish library and supported in turn by the Folk Shule, the Zionist organization, and now by the Saidye Bronfman Centre of the YM-YWHA. And since 1967 Winnipeg has developed an acclaimed performing troupe, the Chai Folk Ensemble, combining dance, chorus and orchestra in perpetuating the Yiddish and Hebrew musical heritage. Archival programs and historical societies are developing, and museum exhibits are entering the scene. The best permanent museum exhibits to this point are probably at the Beth Tzedec Synagogue and the Baycrest Centre for the Aged in Toronto.

Jewish life and tradition has given Canada not only peddlers and politicians, but Cabinet ministers, high court justices, and founders of theatre centres, symphony conductors, musicians and composers, as well as poets, novelists and movie makers, with talents ranging from mediocre to superb.

In spite of all this one must still ask: can Jewish life survive in a distinctive form in the conditions of Canadian freedom? This can only be answered in the Jewish tradition of an answering question. Moses Hess once said, "Jews are the yeast of western humanity." The question is, how long can Jewish yeast work in today's world, in which western humanity (Canada included) is but one member, and no longer superior to any other members, of the family of humankind?

Notes

1.   A number of Jews were living in Halifax as early as 1752. Most of them were merchants who came from the New England colonies. This group completely disappeared by 1810 and a stable Jewish population did not develop in the Maritimes until the late 1880s.

2.   Montreal and Toronto began to get Jewish peddlers and labourers with the beginning of east European immigration in the 1860s and 70s.

3.   Legislation passed by the House of Commons allowing Jews to take the oath according to their conscience was repeatedly rejected by the House of Lords. At last there was a compromise enabling each House to amend the oath according to its own wishes.

4.   During the 1790s in Nova Scotia, Samuel Hart (no relation to the Quebec Harts) served as a member of the House of Assembly for about six years. He was married to an Anglican woman and had no compunction about taking the Christian form of oath on being sworn in.

5.   The best-known of the Jewish members of the legislature before the NDP came to power in Manitoba was M.A. (Moishe) Gray, who sat in the House from 1942 until his death in 1966, representing a North Winnipeg riding for the CCF-NDP.

6.   The Manitoba NDP government took office in 1969 with three Jewish ministers. Saul Cherniack began as Finance Minister and Deputy Premier but resigned from the Cabinet after the 1973 election for personal reasons. He is still an MLA and serves as legislative assistant to Premier Schreyer who took over the finance portfolio himself. Saul Miller began as Minister of Youth & Education, later taking in turn the portfolios of colleges and universities and health and social development. Since 1975 he has been Minister of Urban Affairs with responsibility for the Manitoba Housing and Renewal Corporation. Sidney Green started as Minister of Health, later moving to the Department of Natural Resources and serving as NDP House leader. Green is probably the government's most effective debater.

7.   Dave Barrett's political career began in 1960, when, on being nominated to contest a seat for what was then still the CCF, he was fired from his job as a social worker with a government agency. In that election he defeated the Minister of Labour, Lyle Wicks, an old-time Social Crediter, whose political career came to an end as Barrett's began. Before becoming provincial leader of the NDP, some ten years later, Barrett served in turn as director of the Vancouver Jewish Community Centre and of the Jewish Family Service Agency. Like Saul Miller and Saul Cherniack of Manitoba, Barrett comes from a Yiddish-Socialist family background.

8.   Aaron Hart kept a family record in his prayer book in Yiddish where his daughters' names were listed as Chava, for Katherine, and Scheina, for Charlotte. Yiddish was the language of the Ashkenazic Jews.

9.   Two more noteworthy Jewish festivals are Purim and Shavuot. Purim comes one month before Passover. In observance the Book of Esther is read in the synagogue to commemorate the downfall of the Persian tyrant Haman (330 B.C.E.) who sought to destroy the Jews. Shavuot, the Feast of Weeks, is celebrated seven weeks after Passover and commemorates the handing down of the Ten Commandments to Moses on Mount Sinai. Shavuot also celebrates the harvest of the first fruits of spring. Reform synagogues and some Conservative and Orthodox congregations conduct a confirmation ceremony for their religious school graduates at Shavuot.

10.   In spite of David Ansell's position in 1874 he joined the other congregation a few years later, and during 1892-94 he served as president of the Shaar Hashomayim Synagogue.

11.   To assess the immigrant role during that period it is useful to know that the largest proportionate growth in the Jewish population during the first decade of the twentieth century occurred in Winnipeg

where the numbers increased more than eight-fold, from 1164 in 1901 to 9408 in 1911. By comparison Toronto's Jews increased almost six-fold, from 3103 to 18,294; and Montreal's Jews increased slightly more than four-fold, from 6925 to 28,838. It seems reasonable to suggest, therefore, that the potential influence of the radicals as well as the Orthodox among the new arrivals was greater in the western centre than in the East.

12. Bar Mitzvah is the ceremony in which a thirteen-year-old Jewish boy is recognized as an adult, responsible from then on for his own moral and religious conduct. The boy is called up to read a portion of the Torah for the first time, during Sabbath service in the synagogue. After the Torah reading is concluded the boy then recites the Haftorah, the portion from the prophets which is also read at each Sabbath service. In Europe the young lad would also give a speech displaying his knowledge of the Torah. In Canada this has been modified into a declamation about God, Torah, love of parents, etc. Preparing a boy for his Bar Mitzvah may take three months to a year of special instruction. Even in families where children have not been given any type of Jewish education, particularly in small towns where there are no Jewish schools, when a boy reaches the age of twelve parents will often make special arrangements to give him a crash course in Hebrew sufficient to enable him to carry out the minimum Bar Mitzvah ritual.

13. The move for sexual equality in the synagogue has led the Reform and Conservative congregations to establish a Bat Mitzvah ceremony for the girls which is similar, though not quite equal, to the Bar Mitzvah. The main difference has to do with being called to the reading of the Torah. Until recent years this has been strictly a male privilege in synagogues of all denominations. Most Reform synagogues now call women to the Torah equally with men, and some Conservative synagogues are beginning to do so. Moreover the Reform rabbinical seminary has graduated the first women rabbis, and another seminary closer to the Conservative movement is also accepting women for the rabbinate. In Orthodox congregations, however, women have not yet been permitted to come out from behind the mechitza, the partition separating them from the men, to participate in any ritual from the bimah, the platform from which the service is conducted.

14. Simon Belkin served for many years as director of the Jewish Colonization Association in Canada and authored two works of Canadian Jewish History, *Through Narrow Gates*, a volume on Jewish immigration, Canadian Jewish Congress, 1966; and the *Labor Zionist Movement in Canada, 1904-1920* (Yiddish), Actions Committee of the Labor Zionist Movement, 1956.

15. Lyon Cohen and Maxwell Goldstein were clearly very different in background and character. Lyon Cohen's uncle, Rabbi Hirsch Cohen, was considered the Orthodox chief rabbi of Montreal for many years. Moreover, when Lyon Cohen spoke about doing justice to the individual requirements of the immigrants he demonstrated it in one way be helping several newcomer groups to establish their own congregations. He remained a leader, and later was president of Shaar Hashomayim Synagogue and continued to work with Goldstein in the top ranks of the Jewish community.

16. Lazarus Cohen was the father of Lyon Cohen and the progenitor of the first dynasty family in the leadership of the Canadian Jewish community. Within a few months of his return from Palestine, Lazarus Cohen became treasurer and colonization chairman of the Baron de Hirsch Institute. At the end of 1893 he travelled to western Canada where he was instrumental in preventing the collapse of the Hirsch settlement before the end of its first year. Lazarus's two sons, A.Z. Cohen and Lyon, each served as president of the Baron de Hirsch Institute, as did two of his grandsons, Horace R. Cohen and Lawrence Z. Cohen. The poet Leonard Cohen is his great-grandson. Peter Newman claims that, at the turn of the century, Lazarus Cohen was the second richest Jew in Canada — he was a coal merchant, headed a brass foundry and became active in the dredging business. (The wealthiest Jew must have been Sir Mortimer B. Davis of the Imperial Tobacco Company.)

17. The number of Jews recorded by religion in the 1971 census was 276,025. The number of Jews by ethnic origin was 296,945. Since 1951 there has been a considerable difference in census figures for Jews by ethnic origin and by religion. In 1951 and 1961 the number of Jews by religion exceeded the ethnic origin figure by 23,000 and 81,000 respectively. The 1961 discrepancy was so great that it was finally realized that the method of gathering and recording ethnic origin information was inadequate. The system appears to have been improved, for the 1971 census records the number of Jews by ethnic origin at 21,000 greater than the number by religion. This difference is accounted for by the fact that just under 10,000 Jews reported "no religion" while the rest gave their religion as Roman Catholic, United Church, Anglican or other denominations.

Acknowledgements

My contribution to this book arises from the research and writing of Canadian Jewish history in which I have been engaged for more than a decade. It would therefore be impossible to thank everyone individually who has assisted me.

Primary appreciation must go to the Canadian Jewish Congress, the organization which made it possible for me to undertake this work in the first instance, and to Saul Hayes, Q.C., O.C., for his support and encouragement. I am particularly grateful to the Canada Council for two research grants, to the Memorial Foundation for Jewish Culture for a fellowship grant, and to Dr. W.L. Morton, Dr. Harry Hawthorn, Samuel Freedman, chief justice of Manitoba, Dr. Jacob Marcus and Dr. Lovell Clark who supported me in obtaining those grants.

My research work has taken me to the Public Archives in Ottawa and to every provincial archives from Victoria to Quebec City. Thanks are due to all archives staff members who assisted me and particularly to Willard Ireland and Inez Mitchell (now retired) of the British Columbia Archives, to John Bovey and Barry Hyman of the Manitoba Archives, and to R.S. Gordon and Walter Neutel of the Public Archives of Canada and to Louis Rosenberg for the use of his documentary and pictorial collection. I have also made research visits to and enjoyed the assistance of Séminaire Saint Joseph in Trois Rivières, the American Jewish Historical Society at Waltham, Mass., and the American Jewish Archives in Cincinatti, Ohio.

Special thanks are due to those publications which have published my historical articles in recent years including *Viewpoints,* the Canadian Jewish quarterly; *Transactions* of the Manitoba Historical Society; *Congress Bulletin,* Montreal; the *Canadian Jewish News,* Toronto; the *Western Jewish News* and the *Jewish Post,* Winnipeg; the *Chronicle-Review,* Montreal; and to *The Beaver, Magazine of the North,* and its editor, Helen Burgess, for her advice and assistance toward this volume.

Thanks are due on behalf of my co-author William Kurelek and myself to the Jewish Historical Society of Western Canada and its staff; to Dr. Stephen Speisman, the archivist of the Canadian Jewish Congress in Toronto; to Ann Rosen for her memoir of farm life in North Dakota; and to all the people, too numerous to mention, who have contributed to the pictorial, documentary and oral history collection of the Jewish Historical Society. I would also like to express personal appreciation to former staff associates and particularly to Ann Steindel.

In this my first published work, special thanks must go to my co-author, William Kurelek, to publisher Mel Hurtig, and to Av Isaacs. My heartfelt appreciation goes to my mother and the women of my family who always encouraged my writing endeavors, and to Bertha for her constant and devoted support.

A.J. Arnold

Jewish Life in Canada

Design & Production/David Shaw
Typesetting/Southam Business Publications Limited (Text)
            Techni-Process Lettering Limited (Display)
Colour Separations/Herzig Somerville Limited
Printing & Binding/T.H. Best Printing Company Limited

First Edition, 1976.